The Tumbleweed Gourmet

Cooking with Wild Southwestern Plants

Also by Carolyn Niethammer

American Indian Food and Lore
Daughters of the Earth

The University of Arizona Press
Tucson

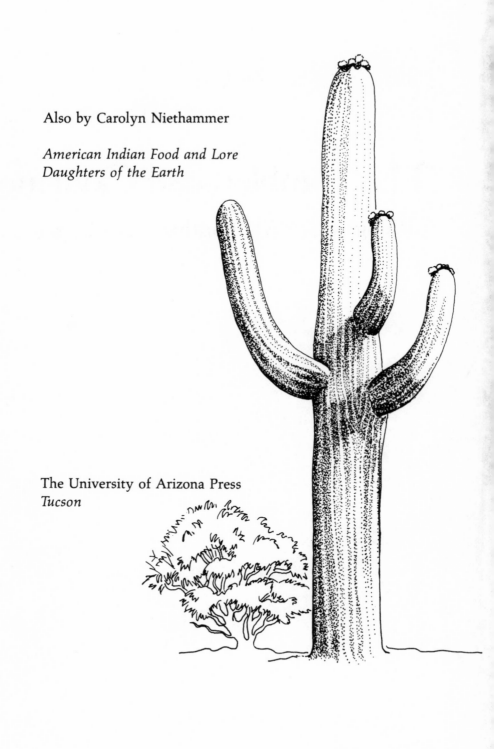

Carolyn J. Niethammer

The Tumbleweed Gourmet

Cooking with Wild Southwestern Plants

Illustrations by
Jenean Thomson

Neither the author nor the University of Arizona Press will accept responsibility for any illness, injury, or death resulting from misidentification of desert plants used in this book. Those readers who elect to gather such plants should take special care to check them against a standard guide to regional flora. State and local regulations for gathering plants, seeds, and fruits on public lands vary widely; readers are therefore strongly urged to seek guidance from the appropriate authorities before collecting. Of course, any collecting on private property must be done with the permission of the owner of that property.

THE UNIVERSITY OF ARIZONA PRESS
Copyright © 1987
The Arizona Board of Regents
All Rights Reserved

This book was set in 11/14 Linotron 202 Aldus.
Manufactured in the U.S.A.

Library of Congress Cataloging in Publication Data

Niethammer, Carolyn J.
    The tumbleweed gourmet,
    cooking with wild Southwestern plants

    Includes index.
    1. Cookery (Wild foods)   2. Wild plants, Edible—
West (U.S.)   3. Desert flora—West (U.S.)   I. Title.
TX823.N54   1987   641.6   87-5948
ISBN 0-8165-1021-0 (alk. paper)

British Library Cataloguing in Publication data are available.

*This book is dedicated to the memory of
my mother and father who taught me to cook
and to enjoy good food.*

CONTENTS

ACKNOWLEDGMENTS

I had a great deal of help gathering the information for this book. Gary Nabhan gave much and freely. Dennis Cornejo, Mahina Drees, Richard Felger, Linda Leigh, Carlos Nagel, Lynn Ratner, Karen Reichardt, Joe Scheerens, Ann Tinsley, Rosa Maria Valdivia, C. W. Weber, and Nick and Susanna Yensen all provided materials, information, and inspiration.

The names of people who shared recipes are listed with their wonderful creations.

Donna Guy, Gary Hearn, Linda Laird, and Bruce Kilpatrick and Ann Schlumberger were gracious and faithful tasters who ate first and asked questions later. They and many other friends and friends-of-friends ate and enjoyed these dishes. Because the editors at the University of Arizona Press joined this project after the recipe testing had been completed, they let my friends vouch for the merits of all the recipes in this volume.

My husband, Ford Burkhart, helped gather the plants, ate everything with relish, washed the dishes, paid the bills, and kept smiling. I am grateful for the help of all these people.

C. J. N.

INTRODUCTION

As the late summer sun gives a golden cast to my kitchen, the room fills with the unusual and unmistakable aromas of a desert harvest. A kettle of mesquite pods simmers gently, releasing an earthy, caramel smell. The pods are softening so that later, when they have cooled, I can plunge my hands into the kettle and squeeze all the sweetness of the pods into the cooking water.

I transfer a dozen crimson prickly pears from a pot in which they have been boiled to a sieve propped over a bowl. As I mash the fruit to release the juice, the spicy, winelike perfume tells me that I am in the desert and it is August. I mash too enthusiastically and juice spatters, making brilliant polka dots on the white kitchen counter.

Every autumn, the fruits of the desert harvest convey a mood of fulfillment. As I pick these abundant wild foods and cook them, I experience a kinship with centuries of past desert dwellers who felt blessed to live here and who cherished the fruits of their desert homeland.

A century or two ago, the Anglos who joined the Indians on the desert had to come to terms with this dry land—its joys and its difficulties. But later immigrants have been shielded from the realities.

Today, it is still a blessing to live here in the western Sunbelt. Winters are mild with a lot of sun, and the problems of the industrial cities are far away.

That is the good part. But a startling truth of the West is finally dawning on the three and a quarter million people who over the last decade have fled the dreary winters of the East and Midwest for the relative comfort of the Sunbelt. These folks, along with several million earlier immigrants, have been learning what the Indians and Mexicans knew all along, a fact so central to the lives of these native peoples that it colors every aspect of their existence: few clouds mean little rain, a dry land, and an ecosystem very different from that in the East.

Of course, everybody recognizes the most obvious contrasts. There are cacti and scrub oak in the country rather than thick damp woods. Arroyos are usually rivers of sand, not water. But unlike the native peoples, most of us have made little effort to live with our arid land. As farmers and householders, we have acted as if moisture were plentiful, gulping up water deposited millions of years ago in underground aquifers; harnessing and squandering the flow in our few major rivers; and fighting over who gets what rights to this limited resource.

For years desert agricultural innovators have been simulating temperate and tropical conditions in arid areas so that they can grow crops unsuited to the natural desert environment. But reality is catching up with us. Lowering water tables and increasing energy costs for pumping water up and out of the ground make it terribly expensive to farm many desert areas.

Economist Michael Perelman writes: "The problem is that agriculture is supposed to be an energy producing sector of the economy. Harvest crops capture solar energy and store it as food or some other useful product, yet the energy captured is small compared with the energy used [today] in the process."

The figures support Perelman. On a typical American farm, it takes about ten calories of energy to produce one calorie of food. In the West the costs are even higher. For example, because of greater water needs, Arizona farmers must pay three times more than other farmers to pump water to irrigate their fields.

Irrigation has also led to salt build-up in many areas, to the extent of taking two to three hundred thousand acres of land out of production each year. One-eighth of the farmland in California—one of the nation's breadbaskets—has serious salinity problems, as does a quarter of the land in the lower Rio Grande Valley in New Mexico. In the northern Mexican agricultural area around Hermosillo, Sonora, which produces much of the winter produce for the United States, salt water from the Gulf of California is intruding into many of the deep irrigation wells.

Ultimately these problems will push up food prices. As a matter of fact, the *Global 2000 Report to the President* states that by the beginning of the twenty-first century, there will be a 100 percent increase in the price of food.

It is a situation that each of us will have to face since the average American eats about 1,451 pounds of food each year.

We, as individual consumers, need to stop leaning on scientists to provide all the answers and to become more self-reliant. Robert Rodale, publisher of *Organic Gardening and Farming*, has written: "As food prices continue their march upward, only those people who can put their homes and neighborhoods to full use as food system centers will be able to eat well."

This means gardening, as 42 percent of American households do, and it also means gathering the bounty of free wild produce that continues to grow throughout the continent.

One need not own a ranch or country estate to take advantage of free, wild foods. I live in a western city of a half million people in an urban neighborhood that has been settled for seventy years. Through the year, with no urging from me, my lot produces seven kinds of edible wild greens, prickly pear pads and fruits, and a large crop of mesquite pods.

Because I have been busy writing this book, I have neglected my yard work. I look out the window this afternoon at a carpet of weeds. But I do not feel too guilty, because I know that even though I used up the last of the lettuce in the refrigerator last night we will have salad for dinner—free—compliments of my weed patch.

Realistically, we cannot expect all the inhabitants of such Sunbelt cities as Tucson, Phoenix, Indio, Albuquerque, and

Austin to head for the weed patch every night after work to gather their supper. Even the early Indians had to give up their reliance on hunting and gathering and supplement their food supply with agriculture as their populations grew.

It is necessary, however, to expand our concept of appropriate agricultural products for arid or semi-arid areas—which, incidentally, is fully two-thirds of the earth's land surface. We often congratulate ourselves on having attained a more varied diet than our ancestors had, but in truth, we have short-sightedly and dangerously contracted our variety of food.

Over the centuries, humans have used about 3,000 plants for food. A much smaller number, perhaps 150, have been cultivated on a commercial basis. Today the number of major food sources is much smaller. Eighty-five to ninety percent of all human energy is supplied by just 15 plants: rice, corn, wheat, sorghum, barley, sugar cane, sugar beets, potatoes, sweet potatoes, cassava, common beans, soybeans, coconuts, and bananas.

Compared with various major food plants of the pre-industrial world, water and temperature requirements for these food crops are critical. None of these domesticated species are particularly adapted to arid lands.

As an example of the potential of an arid area and how it has contracted, ethnobotanists Richard S. Felger and Gary P. Nabhan estimate that the Sonoran Desert alone provided indigenous peoples with 375 noncultivated edible plants—about 10 percent of which were major food sources.

Most of these foods are still grown in the Sonoran Desert. They taste good and are nutritious, but we have forgotten about them.

Our inattention is going to catch up with us.

Felger and Nabhan warn: "The environment and economic costs of supporting ecologically maladapted modern industrial agricultural crops are great: high petrochemical inputs, extravagant water importation projects, fossil ground water pumping, increasing soil salinity, and depletion of soil fertility."

Their antidote is that "crops be developed to fit the environment rather than the environment being modified to fit the commercial crop."

This will be challenging enough in areas that are hot and dry, but it is even more difficult to find something to grow on the abandoned fields that are hot and dry and *salty*. One group of plants called "halophytes" tolerate high levels of salinity. The Environmental Research Laboratory at the University of Arizona, Tucson, has sent a number of botanists out to scour the planet for halophytes that might have potential as agricultural crops for man or beast. The search and the promising plants researchers have uncovered are discussed later in the book. But whether a plant grows in fresh water or salty, developing it from a wild to a domesticated species is more complicated than just gathering seeds, planting, and fertilizing.

Actually, even the scientists working with these new crops acknowledge that as few as one in two hundred plants have a chance of surviving all the problems of development along the path to becoming commercial crops.

Soil and Land Use Technology, Inc., a Columbia, Maryland, consulting firm that did a report on introducing new crops, writes: "The feasibility of introducing a new crop depends not only on solutions to technical agronomic and economic problems, but on the availability of a functioning production-marketing-consumption system."

This basically means that even after a farmer figures out how best to grow and harvest a plant, someone must turn it into food and package it; someone else must advertise it and sell it; and a great many others must buy it and eat it.

Joe Scheerens, who is building a career in the development of the buffalo gourd, believes that the success of each new domesticated plant is based on one of three criteria: (1) it must supply an established product less expensively than any other source; (2) it must supply an established product and grow where nothing else grows—that is, not have to compete for good land; or (3) it must produce a product that no other plant can produce, such as jojoba oil, a unique replacement for sperm whale oil.

Whether or not a potential new crop fulfills any of these

criteria is not always evident until well into the research process. Along the way, money—lots of it—is needed to develop machinery to deal with the new food, from planting to harvesting to product development. Cross-breeding to produce a plant that has a reliable, acceptable yield, grows in a form convenient for mechanical harvesting equipment, and does not drop its fruit or scatter its seed is an expensive process. We are talking about millions of dollars.

Most of our agricultural crops were first domesticated by Neolithic societies. We cannot be sure of the cultural costs of domestication—how many people died eating raw cassava, which is poisonous?—but it is certain that the process was spread over many, many generations.

If we are to cope with our water shortages and keep our dry farmlands in production, we will have to domesticate new crops in a very short time—perhaps a decade. Fortunately, we need not start entirely from scratch. There are a few relic varieties of vegetables that the Indians farmed successfully on the arid lands. Gary Nabhan has spent the last several years searching out these seeds and increasing them, rescuing them from the brink of extinction.

Before hybrids burst on the agricultural stage, these varieties served the Indians well. Nabhan came across a report by an Indian agent who wrote in 1919: "Last year the rainfall was abnormally light yet these arid land agriculturalists, ever fighting the desert which is always seeking its own, succeeded in forcing the desert to yield 300,000 pounds of corn, 1,800,000 pounds of beans, and about $25,000 in value of pumpkin, squash, watermelons and garden truck."

Another Indian agent wrote: "Place the same number of whites on a barren, sandy desert such as they [Tohono O'odham] live on and tell them to subsist there; the probability is that in two years they would become extinct." This probably was not counting on deep-well irrigation, and to be safe, we probably should not do so either, at least not as heavily as we have over the last few decades.

Let's assume you are convinced that we should look to these early adapted varieties of squash and beans—at least for cross-breeding—and that some of the arid-adapted wild plants must move out of the deserts and into our kitchens. You are even willing to harvest some food in the wilds or your backyard or alley. Does this mean that you must throw out all your cookbooks and modern kitchen implements, buy a grinding stone, and resign yourself to plain but nourishing food? Far from it! That is the point of this book.

The foods of the past can fit comfortably into the present and the future. Actually, the seed for this book was planted in my mind by a Zuni Indian woman while I was researching my first cookbook. I was asking her about a special Zuni sauce that was traditionally made by smashing together onions, garlic, and ground cherries on a stone mortar.

"Do you still make that?" I asked.

"Oh, yes," my Zuni friend told me, "but now I use my blender."

After my first cookbook was published, I continued my experiments with the wild foods of the West. Although it had been fascinating to learn how the Tohono O'odham Indians made the sweet mesquite pod into gruel a hundred years ago, quite frankly I was not interested in eating mesquite mush for dinner every day. Mesquite brownies were something else. That was more appealing and more in tune with my own eating habits.

As the Zuni woman had indicated, no rule says you have to use ancient techniques in preparing ancient foods. Blenders, food processors, and slow cookers can make quick work of what took Indian and settler women all day. In other words, it is not necessary to go to a stream bed and pound mesquite beans with a twenty-pound pestle in a bedrock mortar. Just as ancient foods can fit into our modern cooking techniques, so also can they be incorporated into our modern dishes.

The little anecdotes I sometimes share regarding how I came upon a recipe are there simply to illustrate that these recipes did not appear full-blown to me in a dream. I made them up and so can you. If I tasted something or saw a recipe in a magazine or newspaper that seemed like it would be good with one of the wild foods, I tried it; and if it turned out all right, I added it to my files. There is always room for improvement, however, and I hope that the better cooks among my readers will waste no time in doing some tinkering with these recipes.

I am assuming that there is a wide range of people interested in wild foods and new crops, some of whom like the out-of-doors but do not know how to cook very well; vegetarians; folks interested in eliminating fat or eggs or sugar from their diets; gourmets who do not care how far they have to drive to buy walnut oil or how much butter or cream a recipe calls for, just so it tastes great. I am assuming, too, that there are cooks who want to take advantage of the many mixes and convenience foods that make meal preparation easier. Perhaps one day there will be enough interest in the subject to have a separate wild foods cookbook for each of these groups, but for now I have included a variety of recipes to appeal to a variety of readers.

Where it is appropriate, I have also mentioned how a particular dish stacks up nutritionally so that you an use this information in your menu planning.

I hope that these recipes are useful both to newcomers to the West and to settled desert dwellers who thought cooking with desert foods was limited to making prickly pear jelly. Let us all continue to share our knowledge of our arid yet productive land. ·

The Tumbleweed Gourmet

Cooking with Wild Southwestern Plants

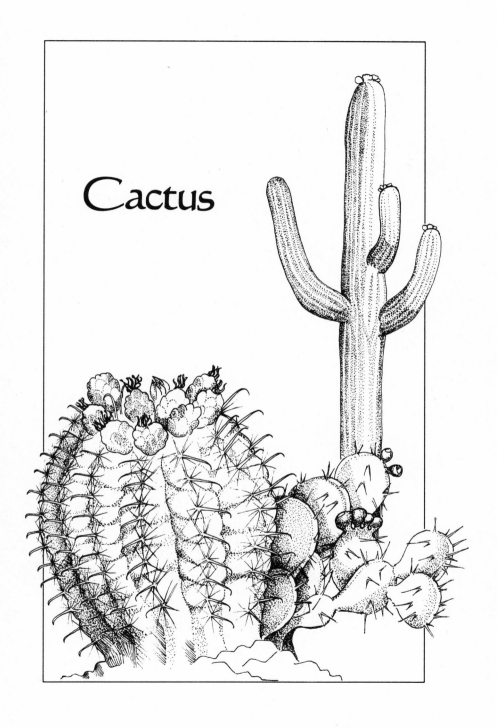

Cactus

PRICKLY PEAR

To the two-legged Desert Rat the spicy, fruity smell of a deep red sun-warmed prickly pear is as much a herald of the coming autumn as the fragrance of ripening apples is to Midwesterners. Native Americans have always considered the prickly pear a seasonal addition to their diet, but for Anglos, its use has been largely confined to prickly pear jelly, a pleasant but unexciting condiment, notable mostly for the fact that it sounds exotic. That is unfortunate, for when creatively used in recipes such as those that follow, the prickly pear is a delightful fruit with a tangy sweetness and an enticing color.

For residents of such far-flung spots as South America, Mexico, Sicily, Spain, and Madagascar, the various parts of the prickly pear plant are still an important food. Practically all Mexicans enjoy prickly pear in some form, and for the poorer classes it is an important part of their diet. In Spain and Italy, the fruit is made into wine. Some Italian residents of New York City pay premium prices for imported prickly pears (also called barberry figs and Indian figs), while throughout the western United States millions of tons of the fruit, far more than the rabbits and ground squirrels can eat, go to waste every year.

It's not only the magenta-colored fruits that are delicious. When properly prepared, the flattened stems or pads are a delicate vegetable. Mexicans on both sides of the border eat them

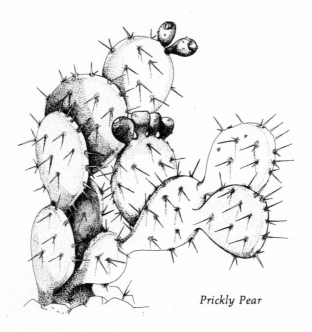

Prickly Pear

often, calling them *nopales*, or when cut into little pieces, *no-palitos*.

Prickly pear plants range from small specimens which spread close to the ground and are covered with spines, to tall, tree-like varieties with few stickers on either the pads or the pears.

About 250 species of prickly pear are found worldwide, all of them originally American. They were taken to such places as Europe, Australia, South Africa, and India as souvenirs by sailors and other early travelers. The first prickly pear plant arrived in Australia about 1839 and has since become a range-land pest of gargantuan proportions. There is even a Prickly Pear Destruction Commission in the Department of Lands in New South Wales.

Because prickly pear plants tend to alter their characteristics according to their environment and because they hybridize freely, it is often difficult even for experts to identify them as to species. For purposes of food gathering it is not necessary to know the exact names of each plant, for all of them are edible.

Some varieties are more desirable than others, but you do not need a botany course to make the distinction.

As for the fruits, if you are planning on making a recipe that requires the fruit in pieces rather than just the juice, look for the larger fruits because they are easier to peel and will give you more pulp for the time you spend in processing.

When it comes to the pads or green portion, the large spineless variety developed by Luther Burbank and used for a landscaping plant is the most desirable. Some common names for this hybrid are Santa Rosa, Sonoma, California, Fresno, and Chico. The large Mexican variety is also easy to handle, but in the United States it does not grow in the wild. Other species have more spines and are more time-consuming to prepare, but they taste fine.

All cactus pads should be picked when they are young and tender during the spring or in the rainy season. The wild variety is ready when it is about the size of the palm of a woman's hand; the domestic varieties can get larger—about the full size of a hand.

(Caution: In some states it is against the law to pick the pads of prickly pears growing in the wild, although fruits anywhere and pads domesticated in someone's yard are legal. Check the laws in your state.)

Both the pads and pears (Mexicans call the fruits *tunas*) are low in calories. Each fruit provides about twelve calories. The pads contain about thirty-seven calories per 100 grams.

Nutritionally the fruits are a good source of vitamins A and C. Nopales provide vitamin A and linolenic acid, which is the essential fatty acid. A generous serving will supply half the needed daily allowance for vitamin C.

Prickly Pear Fruit Preparation

The following directions may appear complicated at first glance, but actually the processes are all quite simple. The instructions are lengthy because I have made the explanations very detailed and have tried to anticipate any questions you might have.

As yet, no one has started marketing cleaned prickly pears. The only way to take advantage of this free-for-the-picking desert bounty is to invest a little time in preparing these fruits. Your effort will provide you with an unusual delicacy of brilliant color and lively flavor.

Three items are essential for working with prickly pears: tongs; good, fine tweezers, and a stiff vegetable brush. You are going to get stickers in your fingers so have the tweezers nearby, use them when you need them, and do not let the stickers become a big irritation, physically or psychologically. David Eppele, president of Arizona Cactus and Succulent Research, Bisbee, suggests that if you wind up with many small spines in your hand, you coat the affected area with white glue. Wait for it to dry thoroughly, then peel it off. I have tried it, and it works on the tiniest stickers better than tweezers. (Archeologists working in Mesa Verde National Park in Colorado found evidence that early Indians were so accepting of the stickers that they even *ate* them, but I do not recommend it.)

Pick the fruit using tongs or wearing heavy gloves. Holding the fruits one by one with the tongs, scrub them all over with a stiff vegetable brush, rinsing them frequently in a pan of water, to dislodge as many stickers as possible.

To Make Juice: Place as many prickly pears as you wish to process in a large saucepan, add water about halfway up the side of the pan, bring to a boil, and simmer over low heat for about twenty minutes. Line a colander with clean muslin or several thicknesses of cheese cloth and dump in the cooked, soft *tunas.* Place the colander over a bowl and mash the fruits with a potato masher until all the juice has drained into the bowl. Four cups of fruit should yield about one cup of juice.

To Make Prickly Pear Pieces: Fill a medium-sized saucepan with water and bring to a boil over high heat. Plunge six to eight pears into the boiling water and cook from ten to twenty seconds. Lift them out with a slotted spoon and transfer to a colander. Spear each *tuna* with a long-tined cooking fork or hold with tongs and peel with a sharp knife. (Don't wait for them to cool; the stickers are softer when they are hot.) Slit each fruit in half and carefully scoop out the seeds with a spoon. If you are short of prickly pears you can reserve the seeds and the pulp clinging to them in a bowl. Add water, and break up the clumps with your fingers. Let the mass soak for thirty minutes, drain off the juice, and discard the seeds. The juice can be used as a pleasant beverage or concentrated by boiling down for use in the recipes. Prickly pears vary in size, but eight to ten pears will yield one cup of fruit chunks.

To Clean the Pads: Use tongs to collect the pads. If you are using the Burbank spineless variety of cactus, you must still clean off the glochids—the little hairs that look so harmless but are really tiny barbs. Boil or steam the pads for about fifteen minutes. When tender, place them one by one on a hard surface such as a plate or cutting board and scrape off the stickers with a small sharp knife, like a serrated steak knife. Cut off the base which is usually tough and one-sixteenth inch around the entire edge of the pad. Rinse the pad and check closely under a strong light for remaining stickers.

The gummy quality in the pads, and to a lesser extent in the fruits, is caused by mucopolysaccharids—a $50 word that you can store away for use when you wish to sound authoritative. These slimy carbohydrates are broken down by weak acids such as vinegar, lemon juice, and tomatoes. Partial drying—either for a few hours in the sun or inside overnight—substantially reduces this gummy quality.

A Tip for Cleanup: Whenever I work with prickly pears in my kitchen I can expect to hear complaints from my husband—the dishwasher in our house—about stickers in the kitchen sponge. I have cut down the protests a great deal by reserving a special sponge—bright pink, so I will remember—for prickly pear cleanup.

Sweet and Sour Mold

Serves Six

It sounds ridiculous, but it looks beautiful and tastes even better. This can be a real conversation piece for a brunch or potluck.

1 can (16 ounces) tomatoes
1 envelope unflavored gelatin
¼ cup prickly pear juice
   (page 6)

3 tablespoons lemon juice
¾ cup water

Empty tomatoes into a bowl and chop coarsely. Drain off liquid using a wire mesh strainer. Measure ¾ cup juice, adding water if necessary, and set aside.

Bring ¾ cup water to a boil in a medium saucepan. Remove from heat, add gelatin, and stir until dissolved. Add prickly pear juice, tomato juice, and lemon juice. Stir in tomatoes. Rinse a one-quart gelatin mold with cold water. Pour in gelatin mixture. Chill about four hours or until firm. Unmold on lettuce leaves.

Brandied Prickly Pears

Makes One Pint

Make these in the fall and store them for the holidays. They make a wonderful addition to your own parties and are terrific for gifts. The recipe can be easily multiplied to suit your supply of prickly pears.

1 cup cleaned prickly pear
   halves
1 cup apple juice
½ cup sugar

10 cloves
1 stick cinnamon
¼ cup brandy

Sterilize a pint jar and canning lid by boiling in water for fifteen minutes. Choose large prickly pears and clean them carefully (pages 5—6, 7). Try to preserve their shape as much as possible. Combine the apple juice, sugar, and spices and boil for five minutes to form a syrup. Add the cleaned prickly pear halves and heat. Place fruit, syrup, and spices in hot, sterilized pint jar and top with the brandy. (If you have too much liquid to add the brandy, return it to the pan and reduce as much as necessary by boiling.) Store in the refrigerator for at least a week before eating to allow the flavors to mingle.

Prickly Pear Kuchen

Serves Sixteen

2 cups prickly pear pieces
   (pages 6—7)
1 cup white flour
1 cup whole wheat flour
¼ teaspoon baking powder
½ teaspoon salt
1 cup brown sugar
½ cup butter

1 teaspoon cinnamon
½ teaspoon nutmeg
1 cup dairy sour cream
2 eggs, beaten
1 teaspoon vanilla
1 tablespoon frozen orange
   juice concentrate

Preheat oven to 400 degrees F. Combine the flours, baking powder, salt, and 2 tablespoons of the sugar in a large bowl. Cut in the butter with a pastry blender or transfer to food processor bowl and process with the steel blade until the mixture looks like coarse meal. Press mixture firmly into an 8—12-inch baking pan. Arrange halved prickly pears on the surface of the crust. Mix spices and remaining sugar and sprinkle over pears. Bake fifteen minutes at 400 degrees F.

In a medium bowl combine the sour cream, eggs, vanilla, and orange juice concentrate. Remove pan from oven and spread mixture evenly over cake. Reduce oven temperature to 375 degrees F. and bake thirty minutes longer. Cool before serving.

Prickly Pear Muffins

Twelve to Eighteen

For this recipe it is very important to make sure every seed is removed from the prickly pear pieces. Biting down on a stone-like seed in a soft muffin can be harmful to teeth.

1 cup prickly pear pieces and juice (pages 6–7)
2 cups flour
2 teaspoons baking powder
¼ cup sugar

½ teaspoon cinnamon
¼ teaspoon salt
1 egg
½ cup milk
¼ cup oil

Preheat oven to 400 degrees F. In a mixing bowl sift together the dry ingredients. In a separate bowl beat the egg; add the milk and oil. Add the wet ingredients to the dry ingredients, stirring only enough to moisten the flour. Stir in the prickly pear pieces.

Spoon the batter into buttered muffin tins, filling them about two thirds full. Bake the muffins at 400 degrees F. for twenty minutes or until golden brown.

Desert Jewel Pie

Serves Six to Eight

This fresh fruit treat resembles chunks of amber floating in a ruby-red sauce. It is especially lovely if you make the pie crust in a fluted quiche pan with a removable bottom.

¾ cup apple juice
2 tablespoons cornstarch
¾ cup prickly pear juice (page 6)

¼ cup honey or more to taste
5 medium peaches
1 baked 9- or 10-inch pie crust

Combine ¼ cup of the apple juice and the cornstarch in a small bowl. Combine prickly pear juice, remaining apple juice, and honey in a saucepan and heat until honey is melted. Add cornstarch mixture and cook and stir over medium heat until mixture comes to a boil and thickens. Cook one minute. Set aside to cool.

Bring a medium pot of water to boil over high heat. Immerse peaches for one minute in the boiling water, then remove with a slotted spoon to a bowl of cold water. Peels will slip off. Slice peaches in uniform slices and arrange pinwheel fashion in two rows in the pie shell.

Pour glaze (thickened juice) over peaches. Refrigerate for four hours before serving. If you've used a pie pan with a removable bottom, take the pie from the pan and position on a pretty plate.

Ruby Port Dessert

Serves Four

This light jellied dessert looks lovely in a cut-glass bowl.

1 cup prickly pear juice
  (page 6)
½ cup prickly pear pieces
  (pages 6–7)
⅓ cup sugar

1 cup water
1 4-inch strip orange peel
½ cup ruby port wine
1 envelope unflavored gelatin
½ cup orange juice

Combine in a medium saucepan the sugar, water, and orange peel. Simmer five minutes. Add the port and simmer until reduced to ½ cup. Remove orange peel.

Soften gelatin in orange juice. Add to port mixture and stir until dissolved. Add prickly pear pieces and juice and chill four hours or until set.

Arizona Sunsets

Serves Four

Be sure to follow the instructions and combine the ingredients in the order listed to get the full effect of these beautiful drinks.

½ cup prickly pear juice
(page 6)
¼ cup sugar
1 quart orange juice

¾ cup tequila or rum
(optional)
4 slices fresh orange

In a small saucepan bring prickly pear juice to a boil. Add sugar and stir until dissolved. Cool.

Fill four tall clear glasss with ice. Fill each three-fourths full of orange juice. Divide liquor between glasses (about 1 shot each) and stir. Add two tablespoons prickly pear syrup to each glass. Do not stir. Cut each orange slice halfway through and hang one on rim of each glass.

Cactus Honey Sherbet

Serves Eight

Your entire kitchen will no doubt have a pink tinge when you are finished making this recipe, but the heavenly flavor is worth the trouble.

3 medium peaches
1 envelope unflavored gelatin
¼ cup cold water
1 cup prickly pear juice
(page 6)

1½ cups prickly pear pieces
(pages 6–7)
½ cup honey
5 tablespoons lemon juice
½ cup whipping cream

Plunge the peaches into a large pot of boiling water for one minute; using a slotted spoon, transfer them immediately to a large bowl of cold water. The skins should slip off easily. Slice the peaches. There should be about 1½ cups.

Sprinkle gelatin over the ¼ cup cold water in a small bowl. Set aside. Combine 1 cup prickly pear juice with peach slices and prickly pear pieces in a medium saucepan. Simmer over low heat for five minutes.

Turn off the heat under the fruit, strain off 1 cup juice. In a small saucepan, combine the juice and honey and cook gently just at a simmer for eight minutes. Add the softened gelatin and lemon juice to the honey mixture and stir until gelatin is dissolved.

Puree the fruit and remaining juice in a blender. Combine with the gelatin and honey mixture and freeze in a bread pan or similar container. When nearly hard, remove from freezer, transfer to a bowl, and beat with an electric mixer. Beat the whipping cream until stiff and fold into the fruit mixture. Return mixture to bread pan. Refreeze until firm.

Either Way Rosy Punch
Serves Twenty-four

Prepare the punch base ahead of time and refrigerate. Before serving, finish the preparation in either the alcoholic or non-alcoholic versions. The tea adds little flavor of its own but helps to blend the other juices.

Punch Base

1½ to 2 cups sugar
2 cups strong hot tea
2 cups prickly pear juice
   (page 6)

2 cups lemon juice
2 cups unsweetened
   pineapple juice

Combine the sugar and hot tea in a large bowl or jar, stirring until sugar is dissolved. Add the remaining juices and chill.

Sparkling Rosy Punch

Add 1 large bottle of chilled lemon-lime carbonated beverage to the base and pour over ice.

Rosy Champagne Punch

Add 1 cup of vodka to the punch base and pour over ice. Add one bottle of champagne just before serving.

Sunset Sherbet

Serves Eight

Not for children, this sherbet rates a spot at the close of your fanciest adult dinner party.

1 envelope unflavored gelatin
1 cup orange juice
¼ cup sugar
2 cups prickly pear juice
  (page 6)

½ cup lime juice
2 tablespoons tequila
1 tablespoon triple sec

In a small bowl, soften the gelatin in ½ cup of the orange juice. In a medium saucepan, heat the other half cup of orange juice to boiling. Add the softened gelatin and the sugar and stir until dissolved. Let cool.

Add the prickly pear juice and the lime juice to the orange juice mixture and pour into a bread pan or similar container. Freeze until mushy. Remove from freezer, turn into a bowl, and whip with an electric mixer. Return to freezer and freeze until almost hard. Remove from freezer and whip again. Add the tequila and triple sec and freeze again until firm.

Dried Prickly Pears

Makes Twenty Pieces

Prepare prickly pear pieces (page 6). Cover cookie sheets with plastic wrap and lay the prickly pear pieces on the wrap. Dry in the sun, protected from insects, or in a gas oven with the pilot light lit and the door slightly ajar (will take about four days).

When the pieces are dry but pliable, carefully peel off the plastic and store in a tightly covered container.

Enjoy them as a snack or use in recipe for Natural Candy which follows.

Natural Candy

Makes Twenty Pieces

½ cup dried prickly pear pieces
½ cup dried chopped dates
½ cup light raisins
¼ cup walnuts
½ cup minus one tablespoon granola

If fruits are not soft and fresh, soften them in a wire strainer set over a pot of simmering water for five minutes.

In a food grinder or a food processor using the steel blade, grind the fruits together (or chop fine with a heavy knife, rinsing it often to prevent sticking). Add the nuts and ¼ cup of the granola and complete the grinding.

Whirl 3 tablespoons granola in a blender until it is fine crumbs. Form the ground fruit into a long roll one-inch in diameter. Spread the powdered granola on a flat surface and roll the fruit rope in it until the outside is thickly covered. Using a sharp knife, slice into twenty pieces.

In the unlikely event that you will want to store this candy, do so in a tightly covered container.

The following recipes were developed by Nancy Weinert for a foods class at the University of Arizona. The recipes use prickly pear puree prepared by a process she developed.

Prickly Pear Puree

Freeze scrubbed and drained prickly pears until hard. Days or months later they can be removed from the freezer and allowed to defrost just slightly. At this point the skins will easily peel off and the flesh will be firm enough to work with. Slit the peeled pears, scoop out the seeds and discard. Reserve prickly pear flesh in bowl. Stir until you have a smooth puree.

(Hint: keep a bowl of lukewarm water on hand to wash and warm your hands.) Work quickly. If you let the fruit thaw too much you will have mush.

Red Rice Pudding

Serves Ten to Twelve

1 cup raw white rice	2 teaspoons cinnamon
2 cups prickly pear puree (see above)	1 teaspoon vanilla
	1 cup flaked coconut
1 package (3½ ounces) lemon pudding	1 cup pineapple, drained
	½ cup heavy cream, whipped
2 egg yolks	¼ cup almonds, chopped

In a medium covered saucepan over low heat, cook rice in prickly pear puree until tender. Cook lemon pudding according to package directions. Cool slightly, then stir in egg yolks. Transfer pudding to a large bowl. Fold rice into pudding along with cinnamon, vanilla, coconut and pineapple. Gently fold in whipped cream and sprinkle top with almonds. Chill.

Prickly Pear Leather

Makes One Roll

Fruit leather is a good item to stick in your backpack for a no-fuss trailside snack.

2 cups prickly pear puree (page 16)
3 ounces grape juice concentrate

2 tablespoons honey

Mix ingredients in a medium bowl and spread on 15 × 18-inch or similar sized cookie sheet covered with plastic wrap. There should be a thin but very even coating. To dry, set in a gas oven with the door slightly ajar for four days. The heat of the pilot light will dry the leather. The leather can also be dried outside in dry weather if protected from insects by screening or netting.

When dry, carefully peel off the plastic wrap and fold the leather into a roll. This operation is more easily accomplished if the leather is warm. To eat, slice or tear off desired amount.

Prickly Pear and Grape Jelly

Makes about Three Pints

2 cups prickly pear puree (page 16)
3 ounces grape juice concentrate

1 package powdered pectin
3½ cups sugar

Sterilize jars and lids by boiling for fifteen minutes. Mix puree, grape juice, and pectin in a medium saucepan. Stir constantly over high heat until bubbles form all around the edge. Add all the sugar at once and stir until combined. Bring to a full rolling boil and boil hard one minute. Pour into sterilized jars and seal.

And now for some recipes using prickly pear pads or *nopales*.

Gazpacho Aspic

Serves Six to Eight

This famous Spanish soup molded into a refreshing salad works nicely with the addition of prickly pear pads.

1 cleaned prickly pear pad (page 7)
1 envelope unflavored gelatin
1 cup tomato juice
2 medium-sized tomatoes
1 cup peeled, finely chopped cucumber
½ medium-sized green pepper, seeded and chopped
½ cup chopped green onion
1 clove garlic, minced or pressed
2 tablespoons olive oil
¼ cup red wine vinegar
Hot pepper seasoning to taste

Mince cleaned prickly pear pad and set aside. In a small pan sprinkle gelatin over tomato juice. Let soften five minutes; then place over medium heat and stir until gelatin is dissolved. Let cool to room temperature.

Meanwhile, peel, seed, and finely chop tomatoes. Stir tomatoes into the cooled gelatin mixture with the cucumber, nopalitos, green pepper, green onion, garlic, oil, vinegar, and hot pepper, seasoning to taste. Rinse a one-quart mold with cold water. Pour mixture into mold and refrigerate until firm, about four hours.

To serve, invert onto serving plate covered with salad greens. Soak a towel in hot water and wring out. Cover mold with hot towel until gelatin releases from mold and settles on greens.

Nopal Frittata

Serves Two to Four

Nopalitos and eggs is a classic recipe for using prickly pear pads. This more elaborate version is tastier.

4 or 5 prickly pear pads,
   steamed and cleaned
   (pages 6–7)
2 small tomatoes
2 thin slices red onion
4 eggs

2 tablespoons butter
½ teaspoon salt
¼ teaspoon fresh ground
   pepper
½ cup grated Parmesan
   cheese

Cut each prickly pear pad into pieces about 2 inches square. Slice tomatoes thinly. Separate onion into rings. Beat eggs.

In a large frying pan with a cover, melt butter and lightly brown onions and prickly pear pieces (*nopales*). Arrange *nopales* on bottom of pan with onion rings on top. Add slices of tomatoes. Turn heat down and cover for one or two minutes to slightly cook and warm tomato. Add beaten eggs. Cook over low heat until just set. Sprinkle with Parmesan cheese. Run under the broiler to brown slightly. Cut into wedges to serve.

Sour Cream Salad

Serves Two to Three

2 or 3 cleaned prickly pear
   pads (page 7)
8 to 10 radishes

½ cup green olives
½ cup sour cream

Chop cleaned prickly pear pads coarsely. Chop radishes and green olives. Combine with nopalitos and sour cream in a medium bowl. Mix well. Serve on lettuce leaves.

Apple, Carrot and Nopalito Salad

Serves Six

In the spring try this new twist on an old favorite.

2 cleaned prickly pear pads   1 cup shredded apple
   (page 7)   Mayonnaise
2 cups shredded carrot   Milk

Cut prickly pear pad into strips ¼-inch wide. Arrange on cookie sheet or flat pan and dry for a few hours in the sun or overnight until the strips are chewy but not hard. Chop into small bits.

In a medium bowl, combine nopalitos with carrot and apple. Dress with mayonnaise thinned with a little milk.

Nopalito Spread

1 cleaned prickly pear pad   2 to 3 tablespoons chopped
   (page 7)   green chiles
4 green onions   2 tablespoons sour cream
½ green pepper   Shake of garlic powder
8 ounces cream cheese   ¼ teaspoon salt
                                 ¼ teaspoon pepper

Mince prickly pear pad, onions, and green pepper using a knife or food processor. In food processor bowl, combine cream cheese chopped into eight pieces, green chilies, sour cream, garlic powder, salt, and pepper. Process until mixed but still crunchy. If mixing by hand, soften cream cheese in a bowl using the back of a wooden spoon. Add remaining ingredients and stir until blended.

Serve with crackers or pumpernickel or stuff celery ribs. Or spread a thin layer over a small absolutely fresh flour tortilla, covering to the very edges. Repeat until all the spread is used.

Roll tortillas tightly and chill for one hour. When cheese is firm, cut tortilla rolls into 1-inch pieces with a sharp knife.

Salmon Nopalito Mousse

Serves Four to Eight

This is especially good for lunch or dinner in warm weather. It is also an elegant first course for a dinner party.

2 large cleaned prickly pear pads (page 7)	¼ cup yogurt
¼ cup vinegar	¼ cup cottage cheese
¼ cup water	½ cup lemon juice
2 envelopes unflavored gelatin	2 green chiles (canned)
½ cup white wine or water	2 green onions
1 can (15 ounces) salmon	½ cup chopped celery
	Salad greens

Mince cleaned prickly pear pads. Place *nopalitos* in a small bowl and soak in a solution of ¼ cup vinegar and ¼ cup water for one hour.

Meanwhile, soften gelatin in wine or water; then dissolve in the top part of a double boiler over boiling water. Cool.

Add the salmon, bones and all, to a blender jar or food processor bowl along with the yogurt, cottage cheese, lemon juice, and gelatin mixture. Blend. Refrigerate in a bowl until very thick but not set. Drain and rinse nopalitos and fold into salmon mixture along with chopped green chiles and chopped green onion.

Rinse a one-quart mold with cold water; add salmon mixture. Chill until firm, about four hours. Unmold on salad greens arranged on a pretty plate.

Sea of Cortez Gumbo

Serves Six to Eight

Gumbos are usually associated with the states which border the Gulf of Mexico, but this one uses ingredients found in and around the Gulf of California (also called the Sea of Cortez). Strips of prickly pear pads substitute for the okra usually used and provide the same thickening qualities.

3 or 4 cleaned prickly pear
  pads (page 7)
1 pound red snapper filets
½ pound shrimp
¼ cup vegetable oil
1 cup chopped onion
1 cup thinly sliced celery
½ cup chopped green pepper
1 clove garlic, minced
1 tablespoon finely chopped
  parsley

1 tablespoon flour
1½ teaspoons chili powder
1 teaspoon salt
1 can (16 ounces) tomatoes
1 can (8 ounces) tomato
  sauce
½ cup water
Dash hot pepper sauce
Hot cooked rice

Steam pads for only five minutes. Cut into 1-inch squares. You should have 1 cup. Set aside.

Cut filets into 1½-inch chunks. Peel and devein shrimp. Heat oil in large deep skillet or dutch oven. Add onion, celery, green pepper, garlic, and parsley and cook two to three minutes, stirring often.

Combine flour, chili powder, and salt and add to vegetables. Break up canned tomatoes and add with tomato sauce and water. Stir until well-combined. Add fish, shrimp, and prepared prickly pear pads, stirring carefully. Bring to a boil, turn down heat, cover, and simmer fifteen to twenty minutes or until fish flakes easily when tested with a fork.

Spoon over hot cooked rice.

Chicken Yucatán

Serves Six

This is a very modernized adaptation of a dish which originated on the Yucatán Peninsula of Mexico.

2 or 3 cleaned prickly pear
  pads (page 7)
5 pounds chicken parts
Small amount of flour seasoned with salt and pepper
3 to 4 tablespoons oil
6 to 7 tablespoons butter
1 medium onion, thinly sliced

2 garlic cloves, minced
1 small can frozen orange
  juice concentrate
¼ cup chopped green chiles
⅓ cup pine nuts, if desired
2 tablespoons chopped fresh
  cilantro or parsley
Hot cooked rice

The day before you want to serve the dish, prepare and clean the prickly pear pads. Cut into thin strips and allow to air dry overnight.

Wipe the chicken sections dry and dust lightly with seasoned flour. Heat the oil and butter mixture in one large skillet or two smaller ones. Add the chicken pieces, browning quickly on both sides. Add the onion and garlic and continue cooking for five minutes. Add the orange juice concentrate, turning the chicken to distribute the sauce.

Reduce the heat, cover the pan, and simmer gently for ten minutes. Remove the cover, add the green chiles, pine nuts if desired, and prickly pear strips (nopalitos). Continue cooking until the chicken is done. Serve over hot cooked rice and sprinkle with the chopped cilantro or parsley.

Southwestern Casserole

Serves Four to Six

8 cleaned prickly pear pads
   (page 7)
3 to 4 cups mashed tepary or
   pinto beans

2 cups enchilada sauce
   (canned or homemade)
1 cup grated jack cheese

Dry cleaned prickly pear pads in the sun or in a gas oven with the pilot light on and the door open for two to three hours or on a plate overnight.

Preheat oven to 350 degrees F. Spread each pad with mashed beans and arrange in a flat casserole dish. Cover with enchilada sauce. Top with grated cheese.

Bake in preheated oven for fifteen to twenty minutes until beans and sauce are warm and cheese is melted.

Nopalitos Italiano

Serves Six

It is not as unlikely as it might seem to include desert nopalitos in an Italian-style dish. Many prickly pear plants grow in that country—and all the Mediterranean—descendants of specimens taken home by explorers of the New World hundreds of years ago. This makes an interesting first course or a tasty lunch.

6 or 7 cleaned prickly pear
   pads (page 7)
2 tablespoons butter or
   margarine
¼ cup chopped onion
1 medium clove garlic,
   minced
½ teaspoon Italian
   seasoning, crushed

1 can (10¾ ounces)
   condensed cream of
   asparagus soup
1 soup can water
¼ teaspoon paprika
½ cup chopped fresh
   tomatoes
¼ cup bouillon or water

Slice or chop cleaned prickly pear pads and measure 2 cups. In a saucepan over medium heat, melt butter, add onion, garlic, and Italian seasoning and cook until onion is tender. Stir in prickly pear pads and remaining ingredients and simmer until heated through.

SAGUARO

The stately saguaro cactus, rising sometimes as high as fifty feet and supporting two or even three dozen arms, has become a symbol of the desert of the American West, particularly when it is positioned in front of a spectacularly colored setting sun.

In truth, saguaros, while definitely dramatic, are much less common than other types of cactus in the United States and grow only in an area restricted to southern Arizona, small pockets in California near the Colorado River, and the northern part of the Mexican state of Sonora. Even within this area they rarely grow at elevations above 4,000 feet and are most often found on the warmer, southern side of rocky hillsides.

I am always surprised at the number of people who have never tasted the delicious saguaro fruit and the many others who do not even know it has fruit, believing that the empty red husks they see on the tips of the arms are a red flower that somehow follows the white flowers.

The saguaro was originally placed in the genus *Cereus* in 1848, but then two cactus-loving botanists named L. N. Britton and J. N. Rose decided that the plant was unique and needed a genus of its own. They named it *Carnegia gigantea* after Andrew Carnegie who had funded much of the research at the Desert Laboratory in Tucson.

In his exhaustive article on the saguaro, Frank Crosswhite writes that some people believe that the real reason Carnegie was so honored was that it was hoped he would provide more money:

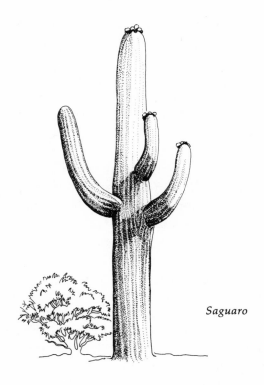

Saguaro

As the story is commonly told, Carnegie was asked to come to Arizona and look at the unusual plant which had been named for him. He obliged and was shown the great forests of saguaro near Tucson. . . . When told that these giants all now bore his name, he inquired innocently how such a characteristic and useful plant had evaded detection near a highly populated part of the state so long. When the blushing botanists tried to explain how it had been scientifically necessary to change the name of the plant and that the cactus had been well-known for many years, Carnegie reportedly became disgusted with a kind of science that could change well-established names of plants to cater to wealthy persons.

In the early years of the growth of the State of Arizona, the waxy white blossoms of the saguaro were claimed as the state flower, but in general the plants were more or less taken for granted. Many thousands of them were thoughtlessly bulldozed to make way for homes whose yards then had to be replanted with something else.

More recently there seems to be a growing awareness among Arizonans as to the value and unique qualities of the big plants, and there are laws to protect them on publicly owned property. Re-establishing a saguaro forest is a very long process. Even after growing for five years, saguaros are only a few inches high; they do not flower until they are forty or fifty years old; and most of the best specimens—those with many arms—are probably about two hundred years old.

Because of this, most homeowners today are proud of any saguaros on their property, build around them, and become quite dismayed if they show signs of damage. Something called "bacterial necrosis disease" (which some scientists claim is not a disease at all but a normal decomposing process) has been a major cause of saguaro death. One woman physician of my acquaintance performed surgery on her rotting saguaro, scraping away the soft part, painting the incisions with Clorox and giving the plant an injection of penicillin for good measure.

Conversely, there are those few anti-social individuals, quite often teenagers, who are so angry with the world they attack saguaros as an ultimate statement of their hurt and disassociation from the rest of the community. If they are caught, they are fined and jailed but that does not bring back the saguaros.

The Tohono O'odham (formerly Papago) Indians, whose traditional home is among the saguaros, used the cactus for building material, fuel, and food. Their year began in the summer with the saguaro harvest and the accompanying wine ceremonial during which they "sang down the clouds" for the start of the life-restoring rainy season.

Their respect for the giant saguaros was so great that they considered them nearly human. Gary Nabhan, in his charming and insightful book *The Desert Smells Like Rain*, reports overhearing a conversation between an elderly Tohono O'odham woman and a boy from the city who wanted to know if one could ever collect fruits from the top of the saguaro cactus by throwing rocks to knock them off.

"No," Marquita replied with a strain of horror in her voice.

"The saguaros—they are Indians too. You don't *ever* throw *anything* at them. If you hit them in the head with rocks you could kill them. You don't ever stick anything sharp into their skin either, or they will just dry up and die. You don't do anything to hurt them. They are Indians."

Saguaro fruits look something like tiny three-inch watermelons: they have an inedible green rind and red flesh inside with a great number of tiny black seeds.

Saguaro fruit provides good nutrition. The seeds have considerable amounts of protein, fat, and vitamin C. Be warned, however, that they are not a low-calorie snack. Each fruit contains about 34 calories and two tablespoons of dried saguaro seed has 74 calories.

Saguaro Fruit Gathering

Saguaro gathering takes a bit of planning to assemble all the apparatus. If you do not live right on the desert, it is fun to make a real expedition of the trip taking along family or friends and a breakfast or supper picnic.

The fruits start getting ripe near the end of June and the harvest can continue through the middle of July. All the fruits on a plant are not ripe at the same time.

If you are planning to collect in any quantity, make your expedition in the very early morning or just before dark in the evening when it is a little cooler.

saguaro fruit

You'll need a couple of small buckets, a knife, perhaps a plastic bag or two, and a very long, sturdy, but lightweight pole with some sort of crosspiece on the end. Two dead saguaro ribs spliced together with a crosspiece fixed to the end with baling wire is the traditional tool and I have not seen it improved upon although I have tried other kinds of poles.

I think saguaro gathering works best in the buddy system: one person knocks the fruits off while the other catches them on the fly with a bucket or net. The reason for catching them is that if the fruit is so ripe that it has burst open, it will pick up lots of gravel if it hits the ground. Throw out any fruit that smells sour or spoiled, no matter how hard you worked to get it. Bad ones spoil the whole batch.

Preparing the Fruit

I usually clean all the fruit from one plant before I go on to the next, slitting open the rinds with a knife if they are closed, extracting the pulp into a small plastic bucket with my thumb, and throwing the rinds to the ground with the red side up. The Tohono O'odham say that helps bring the rain.

Caterer Stephanie Daniel has discovered that fresh saguaro pulp can be frozen in plastic bags. It is then easy to break off whatever amount is needed for a recipe.

Preparing Saguaro Juice and Syrup

When you get home with your harvest, add as much water to the bucket as you have pulp. Plunge your hands in and break up the clumps as much as possible. Cover the bucket with a clean towel, let it stand in a cool place, and wait six to eight hours for the fruit to soak.

When the time is up, use a fine wire-mesh strainer to strain all the liquid into a large pot. Boil the liquid until it is reduced by half for juice; reduce it further for syrup. Store in the refrigerator in clean glass jars, or use in the following recipes.

Preparing the Seeds

Spread the seeds remaining from the juice-preparing operation on a large flat pan or tray and dry them in the sun. There will be some washed out pulp on the seeds and this will dry whitish. When the seeds are dry, break them up. Using a pan with sides at least two inches high, or a bowl, vigorously shake the seeds; the white dried pulp will rise to the top and can be skimmed off until mostly smooth shiny seeds remain. Store the seeds in a can or jar with a tight-fitting lid.

The following three recipes use unseparated saguaro pulp and seeds.

Quick Saguaro Ice Cream
Serves Four

This is nice to put together when you have just returned from a saguaro-gathering expedition and want to make something fast.

1½ cups slightly softened
   vanilla ice cream
1 cup fresh or frozen saguaro
   fruit (page 30)

2 tablespoons frozen orange
   juice concentrate
2 tablespoons triple sec
   (optional)

Combine the ingredients in a large bowl. Beat with an electric mixer or by hand. Pour into a bread pan or similar container and freeze until firm, about two hours.

Quick Saguaro Bread

Makes One Loaf

½ cup butter or margarine
½ cup sugar
1 teaspoon vanilla
2 eggs
1½ cups flour

¼ teaspoon baking soda
¼ teaspoon cream of tartar
¼ cup yogurt
1 cup fresh or frozen
  saguaro fruit (page 30)

Preheat oven to 350 degrees F. Lightly grease a 5 × 9-inch loaf pan.

Cream butter or margarine, sugar, and vanilla in a medium bowl. Add eggs one at a time, beating well. Add baking soda and cream of tartar. Beat well. Add flour, yogurt, and saguaro fruit. Beat until well combined. Pour into prepared pan and bake in preheated oven for forty-five to fifty minutes or until toothpick inserted in center comes out clean.

Saguaro Cake

Caterer Stephanie Daniel has been called on to serve several native or wild food dinners and luncheons and the guests are still talking about them months later. Stephanie's secret of success is to introduce new or unusual ingredients in the context of ordinary, familiar dishes. What could be more familiar than cake?

1½ cups fresh or frozen
  saguaro fruit (page 30)
1 white or yellow add-water-
  only cake mix

1 tablespoon vanilla
2 tablespoons sherry or
  orange liqueur

Preheat oven according to package directions. Grease and flour a fluted bundt cake pan. Combine ingredients and bake according to package directions.

Here are recipes that use saguaro juice.

Saguaro Sherbet

Serves Eight

1 envelope unflavored gelatin
1 cup saguaro juice (page 30)
½ cup boiling water
2 tablespoons lemon juice
1½ cups milk

1 cup heavy cream
1 to 3 tablespoons rum or
blackberry brandy,
if desired

In a mixing bowl soften the gelatin in ¼ cup of the saguaro juice. Pour the boiling water over the gelatin and stir until gelatin is dissolved. Add remaining ¾ cup saguaro and lemon juice. Allow the mixture to cool to room temperature and then pour into a refrigerator tray or bread pan. Freeze until it is partially set, around an hour.

Meanwhile, chill whipping cream, bowl, and beaters. When juice mixture is thickened, transfer it to a deep bowl and beat with an electric mixer until frothy. Beat the cream until stiff and fold the two mixtures together gently until well combined. Fold in rum or blackberry brandy if desired. Return to freezer and freeze until firm, three to four hours.

Desert Dawn Pie

Serves Six to Eight

Slices of this pie will reveal layers of deep pink and rich gold similar to the sky at dawn over the desert. The directions may seem long but the procedure is not complicated.

3 eggs
¾ cup saguaro juice (page 30)
¼ cup sugar
1 envelope unflavored gelatin
¼ cup frozen orange juice
  concentrate

1 cup heavy cream
¼ teaspoon almond extract
4 or 5 drops yellow food
  coloring
1 baked 9-inch pie crust

Separate eggs, placing whites in a small deep bowl and yolks in the top part of a double boiler. Beat yolks; add saguaro juice, sugar, and gelatin. Cook in the double boiler until gelatin is dissolved and mixture thickens. (If you do not have a double boiler you can try this in a regular saucepan, but use low heat and stir constantly. If you are not very careful, and worse yet, if you let the mixture boil, you will have little bits of scrambled egg in your sauce.)

Transfer mixture to a small bowl and chill until it begins to mound slightly, at least one hour.

While the juice mixture is chilling, beat the egg whites until stiff. Whip the cream in a deep bowl until stiff. Fold egg whites and whipped cream together. Transfer about a cup of this mixture to a small bowl and reserve.

Now add the thickened, chilled juice mixture to the larger amount of egg whites and fold together gently. Add 2 tablespoons of the orange juice concentrate and fold together until well combined. Set aside.

Add the remaining 2 tablespoons of orange juice concentrate to the small bowl of egg whites and whipped cream. Add yellow food coloring until it is brilliant and fold it all together.

Put about half of the pink mixture in the pie crust. Add four big dollops of the yellow mixture, then pile on the remaining pink mixture and add any remaining yellow mixture to the top. With the edge of a spatula swirl through the two colors once to make a marble effect. Chill and serve.

Barbecue Sauce and Ribs

Serves Four to Six

First marinate, then bake spareribs in this rosy sauce.

¾ cup saguaro juice (page 30) 3 tablespoons lemon juice
1 tablespoon soy sauce   2 green onion tops, minced
¼ cup corn syrup   6 to 8 pounds of spareribs
¼ teaspoon garlic powder   3 tablespoons corn syrup
1 tablespoon brown sugar

To make marinade combine saguaro juice, soy sauce, corn syrup, garlic powder, brown sugar, lemon juice, and minced green onion. Place ribs in sturdy plastic bag. Add marinade and secure bag with twist tie. Place on plate to catch any drips and marinate at room temperature for one to two hours, turning several times.

Drain ribs, reserving marinade. Place ribs in shallow pan, bone side down. Bake at 450 degrees F. for thirty minutes. Drain off all fat. Pour reserved marinade over ribs and reduce oven temperature to 350 degrees F. Continue baking another half hour or until done, basting frequently.

Five minutes before removing from oven, brush ribs generously with a final glaze of 3 tablespoons of corn syrup.

High-protein saguaro seeds can be used in a variety of recipes.

Arizona Riviera Salad Dressing
Makes About One Pint

This is especially good over a salad of romaine, apples, and red onion slices.

1 tablespoon saguaro seeds
  (page 31)
2 tablespoons powdered
  mustard
¼ cup sugar
¼ cup saguaro juice
  (page 30)

⅓ cup vinegar
1 cup olive oil
3 tablespoons finely chopped
  onion
½ teaspoon salt

Add saguaro seed to blender jar and whirl until ground. Add remaining ingredients and blend until combined.

Creamy Saguaro Salad Dressing
Makes Almost One Pint

This makes a good complement to fresh fruit or gelatin salads.

½ cup whipping cream
1 tablespoon saguaro seeds
  (page 31)
1 tablespoon honey

1 tablespoon saguaro juice
½ cup Miracle Whip or
  similar bottled salad
  dressing

Put whipping cream in a small, deep bowl. Place, with beaters for electric mixer, in refrigerator for about two hours (or a shorter time if you have room in your freezer). Meanwhile, grind saguaro seeds in blender. Set aside. Remove cream from freezer and whip until soft peaks form. In a small bowl, combine honey and saguaro juice; add salad dressing and combine. Fold mixture and seeds into whipped cream.

Quick Saguaro Biscuits
Makes Two Dozen

¼ cup saguaro seeds (page 31)
2 cups biscuit mix
½ cup plus one tablespoon water

½ cup shredded cheese
1 egg yolk
2 tablespoons water
1 tablespoon saguaro seeds (page 31)

Preheat oven to 450 degrees F. Grind ¼ cup saguaro seed in a blender. Combine with biscuit mix, cold water, and shredded cheese in a medium bowl and stir with a fork to form a soft dough. Pat dough into a ball on a floured surface and knead five times.

Roll dough ¼-inch thick and cut with a glass or biscuit cutter. Arrange biscuits with sides touching in a pan or on a cookie sheet. In a small bowl, beat egg yolk and add two tablespoons water. Brush top of biscuits with yolk mixture. Sprinkle with 1 tablespoon saguaro seed. Bake in preheated oven for eight to ten minutes. Serve warm.

Crunch Noodles
Makes Two to Four Servings

6 ounces noodles
1 tablespoon butter

1 tablespoon saguaro seeds (page 31)

Cook noodles in plenty of boiling, salted water until tender. Drain. Toss with butter and saguaro seed.

Saguaro Pilaf

Serves Four

½ cup saguaro seeds
  (page 31)
1 cup bulgur (cracked wheat)
1½ cups boiling water
¼ cup chopped raisins, if
  desired

2 tablespoons sunflower
  seeds (optional)
3 or 4 green onions
1 to 2 tablespoons oil
Salt and pepper to taste

Grind saguaro seeds in blender. Combine seeds, bulgur wheat, chopped raisins, and sunflower seeds, if desired, in a heavy saucepan with a lid. Add boiling water. Cover and let sit for thirty minutes.

Chop green onions and sauté in oil. When time is up, check to see if all water has been absorbed by bulgur mixture. If not, cook and toss with a fork over low heat for a few minutes. Add green onions and toss to combine.

Black Beauty Wafers

Makes Sixteen Wafers

¼ cup saguaro seeds
  (page 31)
1 cup whole wheat flour
¼ teaspoon baking powder
¼ teaspoon salt

1 teaspoon sugar
¼ cup water
1 tablespoon cider vinegar
¼ cup vegetable oil
Whole saguaro seeds

Preheat oven to 400 degrees F. Grind ¼ cup saguaro seeds in a blender. In a large bowl, combine seeds, flour, baking powder, salt, and sugar. Add water, vinegar, and oil and mix, stirring and kneading until a stiff dough forms.

Shape dough into two 6-inch rolls, then slice each roll into eight pieces. For each wafer, sprinkle ½ teaspoon seeds on a flat surface. Flatten the dough and press into the seeds. Sprinkle more seeds on top. Roll with a rolling pin as thin as you can manage—the thinner the crackers, the crisper they will be. Shapes will be irregular. Transfer crackers to an ungreased cookie sheet. Bake in a preheated oven for five to seven minutes.

Desert Health Cereal
Makes Two and One-Half Quarts

Gather the saguaro seeds in the summer and enjoy this hot cooked cereal all winter long.

4 cups saguaro seeds	1 cup wheat bran
(page 31)	1 cup raw wheat germ
2 cups bulgar (cracked wheat)	1 cup cornmeal
1 cup oatmeal	

Grind saguaro seeds in a grain grinder or in a blender a cup at a time. Combine with other dry ingredients and store in an airtight can, preferably in the refrigerator.

To cook, combine a measure of cereal with four times as much water in a covered saucepan. Bring to a boil. Turn down the heat, cover, and simmer gently until cooked, about twenty minutes. One-half cup cereal and two cups water will make two to three servings.

Saguaro Pie Crust I

½ cup saguaro seeds   ½ cup wheat germ
  (page 31)   ⅓ cup oil
½ cup rolled oats   Sprinkle of salt
½ cup whole wheat flour   1 tablespoon apple juice

Preheat oven to 350 degrees F. Grind saguaro seeds in a grain grinder or in a blender. Combine with rolled oats, flour, and wheat germ in a bowl. Add oil and toss until well blended. Moisten with apple juice until it binds together. (If you add too much liquid, the crust will not be flaky.) Pat into an 8-inch pie pan. Bake crust ten minutes in preheated oven.

Saguaro Pie Crust II

Substitute ½ cup ground saguaro seeds for equivalent amount of cookie or graham cracker crumbs in your favorite recipe for crumb crust.

Either of these mixtures can be used as a filling for coffeecake, such as the one below, or crepes, or even little turnover cookies. The first is exceedingly rich and yummy; the second is delicious and sweet without sugar.

Saguaro Seed Coffee Cake

Makes One Coffee Cake

1 package active dry yeast   2 tablespoons butter or
¼ cup warm water   margarine
1 teaspoon sugar   ¼ cup milk
2½ cups unbleached flour   1 egg slightly beaten
3 tablespoons sugar   1 recipe Saguaro Seed Filling
¼ teaspoon salt   I or II (page 40)

In a cup, sprinkle yeast over ¼ cup warm water. Add 1 teaspoon sugar and stir until dissolved. Let stand 5 minutes.

Meanwhile in a large bowl, combine flour with 3 tablespoons sugar and salt. Using two knives or a pastry blender, cut butter into flour until mixture resembles cornmeal. Add milk and egg and yeast mixture to flour and blend well. Knead until dough is smooth on lightly floured board.

Saguaro Seed Filling I

Fills One Coffee Cake

½ cup saguaro seeds
  (page 31)
½ cup almonds
½ cup evaporated milk

¼ cup sugar
2 tablespoons butter
1 teaspoon vanilla
¼ teaspoon cinnamon

Grind saguaro seeds and almonds separately in blender until fine. In a small saucepan, combine ground seeds with evaporated milk and bring to a boil, stirring constantly to prevent scorching. When thick, turn off heat and add sugar, butter, vanilla, and cinnamon. Stir to combine.

Saguaro Seed Filling II

Fills One Coffee Cake

1 cup fresh or frozen saguaro
  pulp (page 30)
⅔ cup raisins
1 cup apple juice

Dash of salt
1 teaspoon vanilla
1 teaspoon grated orange rind

Cook first four ingredients until most of the liquid has evaporated. Stir frequently to avoid scorching. Stir in vanilla and orange rind.

Place dough in greased bowl, turning to coat all sides. Cover with a slightly damp towel and let rise in a warm place until doubled in bulk. Punch down and roll out on lightly floured board to a rectangle 10 × 16 inches. Spread with Saguaro Seed Filling I or II. Roll up like a jelly roll; seal ends. Place on greased cookie sheet; with a sharp knife, make several diagonal cuts in top, about ¼ -inch deep. Let rise until nearly doubled in bulk.

Bake in preheated oven at 350 degrees F. for thirty to forty minutes or until nicely browned. Slice when cool.

BARREL CACTUS

Something about the deserts of the world—perhaps the stark-ness of their beauty—has made them a popular setting for romantic fiction.

But sometimes real life outdoes any author's imagination. My favorite real-life desert romance story concerns Dale Parra, the developer of one of these recipes for barrel cactus and other recipes scattered throughout the book.

Several years ago, this rosy-skinned blonde was working as a nurse in Canada. As winter wore on and on, she and a girlfriend decided to quit their jobs, buy a Volkswagen bus, and escape to sunny Mexico.

After some time, their wanderings led them to the little village of Todos Santos on the Pacific Ocean side of the very tip of Baja California.

There the two young women met a youthful forester named Heriberto Parra—handsome, intelligent, and bilingual. (Mexi-can "forests" are not always pine trees; cactus qualify, too.)

Attraction blossomed between Dale and Heriberto and that led to handholding under palm trees and lots of watching of sunsets over the Pacific. The days were not long enough for Dale, but for her friend—well, Todos Santos does not offer much in terms of entertainment. The friend suggested that it was really time to resume their trip. Dale agreed, reluctantly.

Back on the Mexican mainland, driving around in the bus, it

Barrel Cactus

did not take Dale long to realize that where she really wanted to be was back in Todos Santos. Leaving her girlfriend to continue the journey without her, Dale flew back and married Heriberto. Now the couple have two tow-headed youngsters, also bilingual, and a thriving horticulture business, centered on plants adapted to arid areas. Heriberto often brings desert plants home to Dale, and with her trusty *Fanny Farmer* at her side she manages to whip up something. An example is the following recipe for Bisnaga Preserves.

Because Mexican officials are concerned about feeding that country's rapidly growing population, many of whom are already undernourished, they are looking to wild plants as a possible solution. The Parras have prepared several meals composed entirely of foods of the desert and sea to demonstrate to the movers and shakers the possibilities for using these products.

In the southwestern United States, most barrels are from

about one to four feet high but there are some along the San Diego Coast that are quite flat and ground-hugging. Reports tell of barrels in the Imperial Desert in extreme southeastern California that tower to eight feet.

The scientific name *Ferocactus*, from "fierce," is certainly appropriate for these specimens, for practically every species is covered with tough, sharp, sometimes hooked spines.

For many years the Mexicans have made a candy from the flesh of the barrel cactus, cooking it in a sugar syrup. In some parts of Northern Mexico the barrel has been over-collected for this purpose and is becoming extremely rare. In the United States, there are laws against digging up cactus, although they vary from state to state.

A better alternative is to use the fruits of the barrel cactus which are thornless and have a smooth waxy skin. The flesh tastes light and lemony and the shiny black seeds are easily dislodged. The Indians who lived in what is now the San Diego area used the seeds like grain before the Spaniards arrived. The seeds can be dried, parched slightly in a skillet over low heat, and ground in a blender or grain grinder. Substitute them in any of the recipes for saguaro seed or add them to cereals. The seeds must be ground before use as their hard outer covering is a bit too sturdy for the human stomach.

Finally, what about the myth of the barrel cactus providing a cool well of water for the lost traveler on the desert? A grain of truth, greatly enlarged by myth. To begin with, you need a machete to wack off the top of the barrel—your Swiss Army knife will not do. Once you have laid bare the interior of the cactus, you will not find a vat of clear water, but a soft pulp that must be pounded to release the liquid which is often bitter. You would do better to remember to take a canteen.

Bisnaga Preserves

Makes One Pint

A lovely wine glass filled with these preserves and sealed with paraffin has accompanied the recipe's creator, Dale Parra, to a number of Mexican and international food conferences, where it always attracts much attention.

2 cups barrel cactus fruits

Syrup:

2 cups sugar

½ cup water
4 tablespoons honey

Sterilize jars and lids in boiling water for fifteen minutes. Slice both ends from each fruit and poke out the seeds. Rinse. Place in a covered saucepan, cover with water, and simmer about twelve minutes.

Meanwhile combine the syrup ingredients and simmer for seven minutes. Drain the fruits, add to the syrup, and cook over low heat, stirring occasionally, for another ten minutes, taking care not to burn it.

Pour into a sterilized jar and refrigerate or seal.

Barrel Cactus Chutney

Makes About One Pint

12 barrel cactus fruits, seeded
2 tablespoons salt
2 teaspoons vinegar
2 cups water
1 cup chopped firm pear
½ cup golden raisins
2 tablespoons candied ginger, sliced or chopped

1 clove garlic
½ cup brown sugar
½ cinnamon stick
¼ teaspoon allspice
⅛ teaspoon cloves
⅛ teaspoon nutmeg
1 tablespoon honey

Slice barrel cactus fruit into thin slivers to make 1 cup. Make a solution of the salt, vinegar, and water. Soak the fruit for one hour in 1 cup of the solution. Drain and rinse; repeat the soaking with remaining solution; rinse again.

Combine the fruit and all the remaining ingredients in a heavy saucepan and cook slowly over low heat, stirring often, until thick. (Note: Candied ginger can be found in the spice section of most grocery stores; however, it is more common and usually less expensive in Chinese groceries.)

CHOLLA

The many forms of cholla—some delicate and thin as a pencil, others plump and sturdy—are distributed almost everywhere cacti grow, ranging from Canada in the north all the way to Patagonia on the very tip of South America.

Cholla belongs to the genus *Opuntia*, the largest cactus genus. Its subgroup *Cylindropuntia* distinguishes those species with roundish cylindrical joints from their very close relatives, the prickly pears, whose flat pads have earned them the collective name of *Platyopuntia*.

All parts of all species of cholla are edible: the trick is to choose the tastiest parts of the most desirable types. The recipes given here are for the unopened flower buds and the fruits. The joints are edible also but you would probably rely on them only if you were lost on the desert, and then you would not be interested in recipes anyhow. Some species such as the pencil cholla (*O. ramossissima*) have such small buds and fruits that they are not suitable for gathering.

To fill your basket with the choicest specimens, you need not memorize a long list of species names. On your gathering trips, simply look for the fattest buds and the fruits with the fewest spines.

The flower buds appear in the spring, and when it is time to gather them the petals will be well-formed but still tightly furled and the portion attached to the petals is quite plump. Use tongs

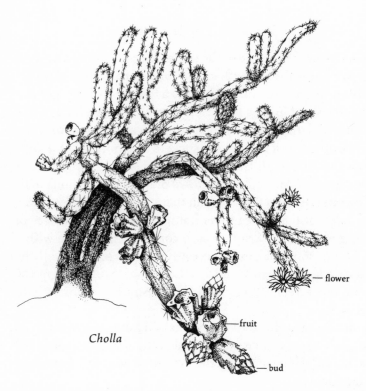

Cholla

flower

fruit

bud

to gather the buds and watch where you step, for the ground beneath cholla plants is always littered with broken sections.

Cholla bud season is fleeting but it comes at what for me is the most joyous and beautiful season, just as the desert is reawakening from its winter browns and grays. Once the spring has warmed and the flower buds have opened, forming beautiful rosettes of every shade from yellow to orange to magenta, the cholla gathering season is suspended until late summer or fall when the fruits have developed and begun to turn yellow.

Cholla buds were and still are one of the prized foods of the Tohono O'odham. They are nutritious too: a 4-ounce serving provides as much calcium as a glass of milk.

Preparing Cholla Buds

The first step is to get rid of the spines. Before proceeding, find a good pair of tweezers, the best you can afford. (Don't skip this step.) Next, if you are processing only a few cholla buds, get two pans or bowls and fill one with clean pea-sized gravel. Put a few of the buds in with the gravel and pour it back and forth from one pan to the other until most of the stickers are knocked off. Finish cleaning the buds with the tweezers.

If you are going to cook for a crowd or stock up on cholla buds for the winter, a faster way to clean them is to use an old window screen that is still attached to its frame, or try nailing a piece of screening to a frame. Prop up each corner of the frame with a brick. Dump some of your harvest on the screen and roll the buds back and forth with a stick. The stickers will lodge in the holes in the screen and snap off. Finish the cleaning with tweezers.

If you are doing this activity in your yard or on your patio, do not forget to spread newspaper under the screen to catch the spines or you will be in agony the next time you walk outside in your bare feet.

At this point the buds are ready to be rinsed and boiled or steamed for about fifteen minutes, until tender. Cooked buds can be added to stews or chilled and included in green salads or potato salad. The one drawback is that they are somewhat gummy, a condition I find undesirable.

I discovered how to deal with that by chance and sheer laziness. One afternoon the remains of a cholla bud and squash luncheon dish sat for several hours in a skillet on my stove, slowly drying from the heat of the pilot light. When I finally faced the cleanup chore, the cholla buds were slightly shriveled. I idly popped one in my mouth and immediately realized that a miraculous transformation had occurred. The bud had acquired a wonderful chewy texture with no hint of the former gumminess.

Subsequent experimentation has shown that the buds can be

quickly shriveled in a convection oven, in a regular oven turned on low, or in the sun.

If you wish to prepare cholla buds for long-term storage, they must be thoroughly dried. To prepare dried buds for eating after storage, soak them in water for at least three hours, then boil for thirty minutes.

Cholla Fruits

Cholla fruits are available for several months in the late summer and fall and are usually used fresh. If you gather a variety which has abundant spines, clean according to the directions given for cholla buds. Slit in half, scoop out the seeds, then peel. Doing the tasks in this order shows you what a very thin shell of flesh the cholla fruit has and reminds you to make the peelings very thin.

Cholla Bud Hash

Serves Four to Six

This recipe is a creative use of leftover meat.

1 cup cleaned cholla buds (page 50)	½ to 1 cup shredded beef or pork
2 medium zucchini	Oil
1 onion	Chili powder
1 tablespoon vegetable oil	Salt and pepper

Steam cholla over boiling water for about fifteen minutes. Drain and spread on a baking sheet in a warm spot to dry until they are slightly shriveled, from one to two hours.

Chop zucchini and onion and sauté in vegetable oil until soft. Add the cholla buds, the shredded meat, and season with chili powder, salt, and pepper to taste.

Cholla Buds and Tomatoes

Serves Four to Six

This is a popular Southern recipe usually made with okra but just as good with cholla buds.

1 cup cleaned cholla buds
  (page 50)
1 can (16 ounces) tomatoes
2 tablespoons butter
1 cup sliced onion
1 tablespoon flour

1 teaspoon sugar
½ teaspoon salt
⅛ teaspoon ground
  black pepper
⅛ teaspoon garlic powder

Steam cholla buds over boiling water for about fifteen minutes. Drain and spread on a pan in the oven or in the sun until slightly shriveled, from one to two hours.

Empty tomatoes into a saucepan and chop into smallish chunks. In a skillet melt the butter and sauté the onion until tender but not brown. Stir in the flour. Add a little of the juice from the tomatoes and stir until you have a gravy. Add the onions and gravy to the rest of the tomatoes along with the cholla buds and spices. Simmer five minutes to heat and blend flavors.

Cholla Pickles

Makes One-Half Pint

If you use cholla buds that have been fully dried and then soaked and cooked, there will be no gumminess in the buds. You can also use fresh buds that have been cooked and partially dried.

1 cup dried and freshened
  cholla buds or fresh buds
  (page 50)
1 clove fresh garlic

1 small red chile
½ cup vinegar
1 tablespoon sugar or honey
3 or 4 cloves

Sterilize half-pint jar and lid by boiling for fifteen minutes. Freshen dried cholla buds by soaking for at least three hours and then boiling for thirty minutes. Drain. If using cleaned fresh cholla buds, partially dry from one to two hours in a warm spot.

Pack hot cholla buds in a half pint jar with the peeled garlic clove and the chili. Heat the vinegar with the sugar or honey and the cloves until the sugar or honey is completely dissolved. Fill the jar with the liquid and cover. Cool, then store in refrigerator at least one week before eating.

Cholla Salad

This recipe leaves plenty of room for your own creativity. You can make a little or a lot for a refreshing summer salad or relish. The proportion of cholla fruit and cucumbers can vary according to taste, but half and half is good. Choose the biggest, fattest cholla fruits you can find to make peeling easier, and pick them before they turn yellow.

Fresh green cholla fruits,	Fresh limes
peeled and seeded (page 51)	Sugar
Cucumbers	Water

Chop cholla fruit coarsely. Peel, quarter lengthwise, and seed cucumbers. Chop in pieces the same size as cholla. Combine cholla and cucumber in a small deep bowl or jar. Add water just to cover. Pour off water and measure. Throw out half the water and put the other half in a small saucepan. Make a mixture of half sugar and half fresh lime juice in an amount equal to the water in the saucepan. Add the lime mixture to the saucepan, bring to a boil, and stir until sugar is dissolved. Pour the syrup over the cholla and cucumbers, cool slightly, then refrigerate for at least two hours.

The following two recipes were developed by Dale Parra of Todos Santos, Baja California Sur, as a means of using some of the bountiful harvest of cholla fruits that are available every summer near her lovely home overlooking the Pacific.

Cholla Marmalade

Makes About One and One-Half Pints

1 cup ripe (yellow) cholla
    fruit, peeled and seeded
    (page 51)
2 cups sugar

Juice of two oranges
1 tablespoon grated orange
    peel

Sterilize three half-pint jars and lids by boiling in water fifteen minutes. Coarsely chop the cholla fruit in a blender or food processor. In a heavy saucepan, combine the fruit, sugar, orange juice, and grated peel. Bring to a boil and turn down the heat so that the mixture just simmers. Simmer for about half an hour, stirring frequently, until mixture is thick. Pour into prepared jars and refrigerate or seal.

Chollate
(Cholla Candy)

Makes Two Dozen Candies

2 cups ripe (yellow) cholla
    fruit, peeled and seeded
    (page 51)
1 cup raisins

1 tablespoon cinnamon
2 cups sugar
Juice of two oranges

Coarsely chop the cholla fruit and raisins in a blender or food processor (or use a wet knife). Combine with remaining ingredients in a heavy saucepan. Cook over medium heat, stirring often until mixture is very thick and able to hold its shape. Set aside until cool enough to handle.

Butter your hands and roll the cooled mixture into a long roll. Wrap the roll in plastic or waxed paper and chill. Slice into bite-sized candies.

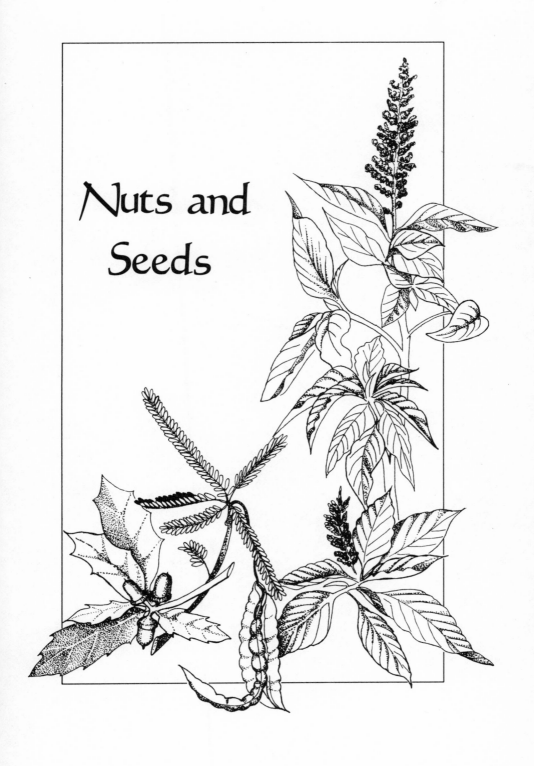

Nuts and Seeds

ACORNS

Balanophagy is a practice that is as western as Tombstone and much older than your great-great-grandfather. If you have not tried it, you are missing out on a gastronomic treat. Actually it is easier to do it than to say it, because "balanophagy" simply means acorn eating.

Acorns, the fruit of the oak tree, have been a popular food of mankind for thousands of years. It is probably safe to say that human beings have eaten millions more tons of acorns than they have of all the agriculturally produced grains combined. In early times, the Japanese, Persians, Sardinians, Spaniards, and Greeks all included acorns in their diets.

On our own continent, acorns were the dietary staple among the California Pacific Coast Indians. Anthropologists speculate that the reason California tribes did not develop agriculture is that by cultivating fields they would have had to work harder for less food than they were able to procure simply by harvesting nature's bounty of seafood and acorns. The Karok Indians of California explained the abundance of acorns in their homeland in a legend which tells of a man who took a long journey carrying only his pipe and a loaf of acorn bread. Whenever he stopped for a snack he dropped crumbs, and acorns grew up.

Tribes in other parts of the West as well as the southeast and northeastern woodlands also ate acorns, although they did not rely on them as heavily as did the Californians.

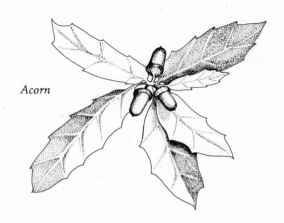

Acorn

In earlier years, acorns were usually ground and made into mush or baked into a hard bread, but modern balanophagists need not be content with such plain fare. Properly processed, acorns can be included in a wide variety of dishes from stews to breads to pilafs.

Generally speaking, acorns compare favorably with grains in nutritive value, although they are lower in protein and higher in fats than either barley or wheat. The high fat content brings acorns in at 2,265 calories per pound compared to 1,497 for wheat.

As is true for virtually all wild foods, acorns have an unusual, earthy flavor, quite unlike anything you might find packaged in the grocery store. Persons who are accepting of new flavors find well-prepared acorn dishes very tasty. In the wild foods seminars I teach, even my most skeptical students begin to show interest when they smell the rich aroma of baking acorn bread. The finished bread, cut while warm into thick crumbly slices and spread with butter, is always devoured with scarcely a crumb left behind.

Picking and Processing

The first step is to locate an oak tree and secure a supply of acorns. They are ready to gather when the shells turn brown and they begin to drop from the tree, from late July in Arizona to autumn elsewhere. The more than sixty species of acorn-bearing oaks in the United States can be classified into roughly two groups: the white oaks which produce crops of mild-tasting acorns each year and the black oaks which take two years to mature a crop of acorns which are usually quite bitter. It is not necessary to be a botanist and know in which group a particular tree belongs; the taste test is sufficient to tell you which are the best acorns in your neighborhood.

Shelling is best accomplished by the old-fashioned smash-and-pick method. Gently crack the shells of the acorns with a hammer on a reasonably clean surface, then separate the meats from the shell. A tiny hole in an acorn shell means that a worm got to that nut before you did. Save your time and toss it out.

The next step is to process or leach the acorns to rid them of their tannin, a substance which is toxic in quantity and makes the acorns very bitter. The Emory Oak (also known as *bellota*) grows in Texas, New Mexico, and Arizona and produces small acorns so sweet that they can be eaten without leaching. Several other types, such as those produced by the White Oaks (*Quercus alba*) are sweet enough so that a few eaten raw cause no ill effects. But most acorns must be leached using one of the methods described below, especially if you are planning on eating a lot of them.

The Indians used to build a nest of twigs near a running stream and pour water over the meal until it was sweet, but this is very time consuming.

Gary Lincoff, who has taught wild-foods-gathering classes in New York City, taught me a method more convenient for the urban gatherer. Lincoff boils the nutmeats, changing the water every fifteen minutes or so as it becomes rust colored from the tannin. Acorns which are not terribly bitter will be ready after a half-hour's boiling and one change of water. More bitter varieties may take up to two and a half hours and many changes of water. Lincoff uses a double-pot spaghetti cooker for this operation, lifting the acorns with the inner pot (which has holes) and discarding the tannin-filled water which remains in the outer pot.

This hot water method dissolves some of the fat from the acorns. Indian tribes who lived in the southeastern part of our country used this boiling method as a means of extracting the acorn oil which they then rubbed on their bodies. To these people, the acorn was second only to hickory nuts as a source of oil.

A third method of ridding the acorns of tannin is similar to that used in processing olives. Soak the acorns in one gallon of boiling water and two tablespoons of lye for twenty-four hours. Carefully rinse the acorns and soak in clean water for twenty-four hours. Repeat the second step two more times. Next soak the acorns in strong salt water (four cups per gallon) for another twenty-four hours. This is a modern adaptation of the process used by the northeastern tribes who leached their acorns with wood ashes.

The final step in all of the above processes is to dry the meal or nutmeats on trays in the sun or in a 100−150 degree F. oven. When the nuts are completely dry, grind in a food mill, blender, or grain grinder.

If you pass the resulting product through a sieve, you will be able to separate the very fine meal from the coarser chunks. The finer meal can be used like flour in the recipes below or incorporated into your own favorite recipes. The coarser bits can be treated like rice or grain in casseroles or used whenever a recipe calls for chopped nuts.

Pickled Acorns

Makes One Pint

2 cups whole processed acorns
   (pages 60−62)
5 or 6 peppercorns
1 bayleaf

⅛ teaspoon mustard seeds
½ cup vinegar
1 teaspoon honey

Sterilize a pint jar and lid by boiling for fifteen minutes. Pack the leached acorns and the spices in sterilized jar. Heat the vinegar and honey until the honey is dissolved. Add to the jar. Add boiling water until the acorns are covered. Seal with a canning lid and store in the refrigerator at least two months before eating.

Acorn Burgers

Makes Four to Five Patties

I first got in touch with Gary Lincoff, originator of this recipe, many years ago after James Beard ran this recipe in his column.

½ cup coarse ground acorn
   meal (pages 60–62)
1 cup water
1 teaspoon salt
1 tablespoon butter or
   margarine

1 onion, chopped
1 egg
Oil

Combine acorn meal, water, and salt in a saucepan. Bring to a boil and simmer covered for fifteen minutes, stirring occasionally. Melt butter in a skillet. Add chopped onion and cook until wilted. Combine the onions, egg, and cooked acorn meal in a mixing bowl. Season to taste with salt and pepper and mix well. Mold into patties. Heat a little oil in a covered frying pan. Fry patties on both sides about five minutes in a covered pan.

Acorn Burritos

Makes Four Servings

This recipe is from Amalia (Molly) Ruiz Clark's book of family dishes called Special Mexican Recipes. Molly was nearing retirement age when, at the urging of her children, she wrote this book. It has been very popular and has led this charming lady to a new career as a teacher in a community college and at a cooking school. Molly remembers this recipe from her own childhood in southern Arizona.

⅓ cup processed acorns
  (pages 60−62)
  or fresh Emory acorns
  (*bellotas*)

2 small flour tortillas
½ cup melted butter
⅓ cup brown sugar
Oil for frying

Grind acorns in a blender until they are fine. Brush the flour tortillas with melted butter and sprinkle on the brown sugar and ground acorns. Roll up the tortillas, turning in the edges; fasten with toothpicks if desired. Deep fry in hot oil until golden and drain on paper towels. Cut in half to serve.

Acorn Muffins

Makes One Dozen Muffins

This recipe makes a rather dark, heavy muffin that is very good served with butter and honey or orange marmalade.

½ cup acorn meal
  (pages 60−62)
½ cup wheat bran
1 cup whole wheat flour
1¼ teaspoons baking soda
Sprinkle of salt

1 egg
3 tablespoons oil
¼ cup honey
1 cup buttermilk

Preheat oven to 400 degrees F. Grease muffin cups. Combine acorn meal, wheat bran, flour, baking soda, and salt in a medium bowl; mix well. In another bowl beat egg; add oil, honey, and buttermilk and combine. Add wet ingredients to the dry mixture and stir lightly until just combined. Do not beat. Spoon into greased muffin cups and bake in preheated oven for about twenty minutes.

Instant Acorn Cookies

Makes About Six Dozen

If you are planning a family camping trip near oaks during acorn season, pack the ingredients for these cookies which require no oven and send the kids out gathering.

1 cup processed acorns
   (pages 60−62)
   or fresh Emory acorns
   (*bellotas*)
3 cups quick oatmeal
1 cup flaked coconut

2 cups sugar
3 tablespoons cocoa or carob
½ cup milk
½ cup (1 stick) margarine
1 teaspoon vanilla

Combine acorns, oatmeal, and coconut in large bowl. Bring remaining ingredients to boil in a saucepan or Number 10-sized can. As soon as the syrup boils, pour at once over the dry ingredients. Mix thoroughly with spoon or hands. Drop on waxed paper and allow to dry briefly, if you can wait!

MESQUITE

The mesquite tree has stirred up an amazing amount of controversy in the Southwest during the last decade or so. Ranchers, disgusted with the trees' invasive take-over habits, have bulldozed them and sprayed them with deadly herbicides. Environmentalists, wood gatherers, and bee-keepers are lobbying to save the trees, lauding them as natural habitats for birds, producers of hard, clean-burning wood, and a source of sweet pollen very attractive to bees.

Then the nation's professional and backyard barbecue fans from Oregon to New Jersey to Georgia discovered from Southwesterners the gourmet delights of mesquite smoke and the distinctive flavor it gives to grilled meats. The pungent aroma of burning mesquite, once the exclusive privilege of cowboys, ranchers, and campers, began to waft over the land. Mesquite chips became a Texas export item.

Scarcely heard above the roar is the voice of a handful of wild food enthusiasts who see the mesquite tree and its bounty of sweet pods as a potential new food crop for water-short farms.

A hundred years ago the mesquite tree was not an issue but a partner in the life of the desert Indians. As one ethnobotanist described it, the mesquite was equivalent to an early K-Mart. The tree provided food, fuel, shelter, weapons, tools, fiber, medicine, hair dye, and other practical and aesthetic needs. For many Indians it was their dietary staple—mesquite mush is

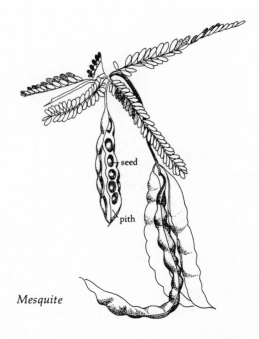

Mesquite

what they ate twice a day, supplemented by whatever game and plant foods they had gathered recently.

Other people besides the Indians have used the mesquite in times of food shortages. One source reports that in the 1800s settlers along the San Pedro Valley in Arizona relied on mesquite pods during times of Apache raids, and later, in the depression of the 1930s, mesquite nourished some people who might otherwise have gone hungry. Even today some residents of Sonora, Mexico, harvest the pods which they call *la pechita*.

There were several reasons for the popularity of mesquite. For one thing, it tastes good—fruity and caramel-like all in one. Also it was reliable. Even in years of drought, mesquite trees produced a crop of tasty pods.

Botanists tell us that there are two major classes of wild edible plants in arid lands: the unfailing crops and the facultative crops which do not produce if it is too hot, too dry, or too cold. Mesquite is the most widespread of the unfailing wild crops in the hot lowlands of southwestern North America.

Table 1. Nutritional Analysis of Mesquite

Component	Whole Pod (100%)	Pith or Pulp (58% of Whole Pod)	Kernels or Seeds (13.9% of Whole Pod)
Crude Protein	14.7	10.5	37.2
Fat	3.2	2.7	6.3
Ash	5.5	6.4	7.6
Carbohydrates	46.3	45.7	32.1
Sucrose	21.3	21.3	—
Inedible Fiber	9.0	13.4	16.8

Adapted from: 1983, F. R. Del Valle, M. Escobedo, M. J. Munoz, R. Ortega and H. Bourges, Chemical and Nutritional Studies on Mesquite Beans (*Prosopis juliaflora*), *Journal of Food Science*, Vol 48, 914–919.

Perhaps most important of all, mesquite is nutritious. Mesquite pods are good sources of calcium, manganese, potassium, iron, and zinc. Although the protein content of the pithy part is low compared to common cereal grains such as barley, wheat, and rice, the seed is about 40 percent protein, almost twice as high as most common legumes. Because it is relatively high in lysine, mesquite combines well with other grains which are usually low in this amino acid.

Growing Mesquite

While working at the Arizona-Sonora Desert Museum, ecologist Dennis Cornejo did some field investigations on the productivity of mesquite trees and found that some of the larger, well-established trees may have as many as 15,000 to 25,000 pods each year. When he fed this information into a complicated mathematical formula, he was able to determine that a theoretical orchard of mesquite would produce an economically acceptable yield per acre of land. Artificial selection and breeding could certainly improve the figures.

Mesquite has a growing number of enthusiasts in the scientific community. Among them is Robert Becker of the USDA Western Regional Research Center in Berkeley, California, who has published a number of papers detailing his considerable research on the processing and nutritive value of mesquite. Even

Europeans are catching mesquite fever. Daniel Meyer and Hans Neukom of the Swiss Federal Institute of Technology have collaborated on mesquite research and several French investors are interested in contributing funds to research and development.

Eventually, however, it will probably take some giant such as General Foods, to provide the millions of dollars it will require to place mesquite cereal or pancake mix on the grocery store shelves.

But we need not wait for Betty Crocker to wave her magic spatula before we enjoy mesquite. Although not as common elsewhere as in the hot deserts, mesquite trees grow from the northern boundary of Oklahoma all the way into South America. They are also found in the Mediterranean area, in Africa, Asia, and southern Europe. I have even seen several on the island of Hawaii. Mesquite occupies 70 million acres in the southwestern United States alone.

Mesquites grow as bushes or trees and are easily recognized from midsummer to fall by the numerous clumps of straw-colored pods hanging among the green leaves. They should not be confused with palo verde trees which are about the same size but have green bark instead of brown and generally shed their leaves in summer. The palo verde has smaller pods which contain edible beans, but the flavor is not at all similar to mesquite.

The most common species of mesquite in the United States are *Prosopis velutina*, often called velvet mesquite and usually found in California and Arizona, and *P. glandulosa*, or honey mesquite, which grows in New Mexico through Texas to the Gulf coast. They are both equally valuable, and food gatherers

need not be concerned with identification. Some pods are striped with red, and some think that these tend to be sweeter.

Eating Mesquite

Because mesquite pods have the shape and size of a green bean they are often called mesquite "beans," which has caused some misunderstanding of how the fruit is used.

Not all of the mesquite pod is edible—a great deal of it is indigestible fiber. The most accessible edible portion of the pod is the pulp or pith between the brittle outside and the hard seeds. Ordinary bean pods do not have this pith. This portion has a very sweet, brown-sugary flavor and can be ground into a meal for use in baking. The pith surrounds a number of stone-hard seeds, inside of which are found the protein-rich embryos or true seeds.

It is almost impossible to crack the hard seed coats with home methods; however, in the past, Indians who lived in the desolate Pinacate Mountains on the Mexican-American border devised a stone implement, given the name "gyratory crusher" by its discoverer, archaeologist Julian Hayden. It looks like a grinding stone with a hole through it and for years investigators thought the artifacts they found were just worn-out grinding stones, or *metates*. But Hayden surmised the hole had a purpose. As it turns out, when a heavy wooden pestle is manipulated in these stones, the mesquite seeds can be cracked, an ingenious bit of technology invented by protein-hungry people.

A modern-day equivalent of the gyratory crusher is a fairly common piece of farm and milling equipment called a hammer-mill. A hammermill can crush and grind both the pith and the seeds of mesquite pods and sift out most of the debris automatically. People who can beg or talk their way into the use of one of these machines can provide themselves with great quantities of high-protein mesquite meal with little effort. Barring that, the alternative is to use one of the methods below and be prepared for a somewhat less nutritious product.

Gathering and Storing Mesquite

Mesquite pods should be picked when they are plump and golden. The flavor seems to vary from tree to tree, some being sweeter than others.

The major difficulty in storing mesquite pods is the tiny grey bruchid beetle. It is so common that most Indian groups accepted it as inevitable—even desirable. However, American desert dwellers do not eat insects these days. Students in the ethnobotany class of Tucson high school biology teacher David Thomas have discovered that giving the pods or meal a quick zap in a microwave oven kills the beetles—a very modern remedy for an old problem. After being treated, the pods should be stored in a tightly covered can.

Processing Mesquite

The trick here is to extract the nutritious edible portion of the mesquite pod from the indigestible fiber. There are basically two ways of turning brown-sugary tasting mesquite pods into edible food: the dry method and the wet method. The dry method produces mesquite meal. The wet method involves mashing the pulp into a sweet liquid, and the directions are below under Basic Mesquite Broth.

Mesquite Meal
(Dry Method)

The first step in the dry method is to toast the mesquite pods in the oven. The pods have a tendency to soak up any moisture in the atmosphere; this trait combined with their high sugar content makes them sticky and gummy when ground unless thoroughly dried. Spread them on cookie sheets and toast in a 125 degree F. oven anywhere from thirty minutes to several hours, depending on how moist the pods are. They are ready when they give a good crisp snap. Grind them right away or they will start absorbing moisture again.

This is the point at which you take the pods to the hammer-mill, but assuming you cannot get to one, use a strong blender instead. Break the pods into small pieces and grind by whizzing one-half cup at a time. You can also use a manual grain grinder or meat grinder. Sift the meal through a fine sieve. Discard the fiber and seeds. Sift again through a tea strainer if you want a very fine product. (A powerful enough blender will grind a few of the seeds as well as the pith, producing a meal with a higher protein content.)

Charles Weber, a food scientist who has studied mesquite extensively, believes it is helpful to freeze the mesquite pods after they have been toasted. He and his assistants have even resorted to using small chips of dry ice to keep the pods very cold and crisp during the grinding process.

The perfect home grinding method has not yet been discovered. However, I have great confidence in human ingenuity, and I have no doubt that a reader of this book will start puttering around and come up with something that works even better than the suggestions given here.

Basic Mesquite Broth
(Wet Method)

This sweet, caramel-like broth is the basis for many delicious recipes, some of which are given here; many you will discover on your own.

4 cups broken mesquite pods   8 cups water

Place the broken mesquite pods in a large pot, cover with the 8 cups of water, cover, and boil for one hour. Cool. Wring and tear the pods in the broth, stirring and mashing the sweet pith into the liquid. Or put one cup of the pods and just a little of the broth into a food processor fitted with a steel blade and whirl until the pods are shredded. Repeat until all pods are shredded. Return the material to the broth and stir. The object is to get as much of the pulp into the broth as possible. Drain off the liquid and discard the fiber. Simmer the liquid uncovered until reduced to 3 cups.

Mesquite Crackers

Makes Six Dozen

These crackers taste so good and travel so well that they have journeyed to several international conferences on the development of new commercial food resources as testimony to the potential of the mesquite pod.

1¼ cups whole wheat flour
1 cup mesquite meal
  (pages 71–72)
½ cup cornmeal

¼ cup vegetable oil
½ cup water
2 teaspoons salt
¼ cup finely ground
  sunflower seeds

Preheat oven to 400 degrees F. Lightly grease a cookie sheet. Combine all ingredients in a large bowl. Mixture will be crumbly.

Roll out dough very thin, working with only a small amount of dough at a time. Cut into 2-inch circles (a juice glass works well). Bake on a prepared cookie sheet in preheated oven. After about four minutes the crackers will begin to brown on the bottom. Remove from the oven, turn each one over with a spatula, and bake another two minutes. Watch them closely. If they become over-browned, they taste bitter.

Mesquite Pie Crust

Substitute ½ cup finely ground mesquite meal (pages 71–72) for ½ cup graham crackers or cookie crumbs in your favorite crumb crust recipe.

Mesquite Apple Loaf

Makes One Loaf

This recipe can make either a bread or a cake depending on whether you add sugar.

½ cup margarine
⅔ cup brown sugar (for cake)
2 eggs
1 tablespoon vanilla
1 cup mesquite meal
  (pages 71–72)
1 cup whole wheat flour
½ teaspoon baking powder

1¼ teaspoons baking soda
1 teaspoon allspice
¼ teaspoon salt
1 cup yogurt
1 cup finely shredded apple
  (about 2 apples)
½ cup nuts (optional)

Preheat oven to 350 degrees F. Grease and flour a loaf pan. In a large bowl, cream the margarine. Add the brown sugar if making a cake. Add eggs and vanilla and continue beating until fluffy. Add flour, mesquite meal, baking powder and soda, salt and allspice. When well-combined, stir in yogurt and apple.

Pour into prepared loaf pan and bake in preheated oven for forty-five to fifty minutes or until a toothpick inserted in the center comes out clean. Cool in the pan ten minutes; turn out on a rack to cool completely.

Popovers de Carlos

Makes Ten to Twelve Popovers

Carlos Nagel, a dedicated promoter of mesquite as a food of the future, developed this recipe.

⅓ cup mesquite meal
  (pages 71–72)
⅔ cup white flour
¼ teaspoon salt

2 large eggs
1 cup milk
1 tablespoon melted butter
  or shortening

Preheat oven to 400 degrees F. Grease popover pans or large muffin tins. In a medium bowl, combine flours and salt. Beat eggs in separate bowl until frothy; add milk and melted butter. Stir liquid ingredients slowly into dry ingredients and beat just until well blended. Pour batter into heated pans, filling them about half full. Bake on center rack at 400 degrees for about forty minutes.

Apple Nut Muffins

Makes One Dozen Muffins

While some scientists are plotting how to do away with mesquite trees, Texas soil chemist Peter Felker is encouraging the use of these sturdy trees for making fine furniture and other craft items. The following recipe was contributed to this book by Pam Felker. This recipe has been a favorite in the Felker household.

½ cup mesquite meal
   (pages 71–72)
½ cup whole wheat flour
½ cup all-purpose flour
2 teaspoons baking powder
¼ teaspoon salt
6 tablespoons sugar

1 cup chopped unpeeled
   apple
2 eggs
1 teaspoon vanilla
½ cup evaporated milk
⅓ cup oil
¼ cup chopped nuts

Preheat oven to 350 degrees F. Lightly grease muffin cups. Combine mesquite meal, flours, baking powder, salt, sugar, and chopped apple in a large bowl. Crack eggs into another bowl and beat; add vanilla, evaporated milk, and oil. Add half of the milk and egg mixture to the flour mixture and combine. Add remaining liquid and mix just until blended; do not beat. Pour into prepared muffin cups and bake in preheated oven about twenty-five minutes.

Desert Cake
Makes One 8- or 9-inch Layer

Neither sugar nor honey is needed to sweeten this cake. The dates and mesquite meal provide enough natural sugar for any sweet tooth.

1 cup chopped dates
½ cup boiling water
1 large orange
¼ cup margarine
1 egg
1 cup whole wheat flour

1 cup fine mesquite meal
   (pages 71–72)
1¼ teaspoon baking
   powder
¼ teaspoon salt

Place dates in a small bowl, add ½ cup boiling water, and let stand for at least one hour (can be done a day ahead). Whirl in a blender to a puree.

Preheat oven to 350 degrees F. Lightly grease an 8- or 9-inch square pan. Grate the rind of the orange and add to date mixture. Squeeze ½ cup juice; set aside.

In a large bowl, beat together margarine and egg. Add date mixture. Combine flour, mesquite meal, baking powder and salt in a medium bowl; add alternately with orange juice to wet mixture. Pour into prepared pan and bake in preheated oven for approximately forty-five minutes.

If you wish to frost, use a mixture of cream cheese, chopped dates softened with a little water, grated orange rind, and orange juice.

Granola Brownies
Makes Two Dozen Bars

These bars require only one-fourth to one-third the amount of sugar in ordinary brownies, making them good for lunch-boxes or snacks.

½ cup margarine
½ cup brown sugar
1 cup whole wheat flour
1 cup mesquite meal
  (pages 71–72)

1 cup granola (commercial
  or homemade)
2 teaspoons baking powder
2 eggs, beaten
1 tablespoon vanilla

Preheat oven to 350 degrees F. Lightly grease a 9 × 13-inch baking pan. Over low heat, melt margarine in saucepan. Remove from heat and stir in brown sugar; set aside.

In a bowl stir together flour, mesquite meal, granola, and baking powder. Add beaten eggs and vanilla to sugar and butter mixture and combine. Add flour mixture and stir again. Spread batter in prepared pan. Bake in preheated oven for twenty to twenty-five minutes or until pick inserted in center comes out clean.

Mesquite Hotcakes
Makes Twenty Four-Inch Cakes

This recipe was developed by Mabel Phillips of Green Valley, Arizona, while she was volunteering at the Arizona-Sonora Desert Museum. Mrs. Phillips suggests the hotcakes be served with honey and butter melted together.

1½ cups flour
3 tablespoons sugar
½ teaspoon salt
3 tablespoons baking powder
2 eggs

7 tablespoons oil
2 cups milk
½ cup mesquite meal
  (pages 71–72)

Sift together into a bowl flour, sugar, salt, and baking powder. Set aside. In a large bowl, beat together eggs, oil, and milk. Stir in mesquite meal. Stir in flour mixture (batter will be lumpy). Add milk if you wish to have a thinner batter. Fry on heated grill.

Holiday Bars

Makes Four Dozen Bars

This recipe is good any time of the year, but is especially appropriate for Christmas. You can bake these bars in November when you have time and store them in a closely covered tin until the busy holidays. The candied fruit may be a commercial mixture or your own concoction of candied citrus peels, cherries, pineapple, dates, and raisins.

1 cup honey	1 tablespoon baking powder
¼ cup water	2 teaspoons cinnamon
3 tablespoons margarine	¼ teaspoon cloves
2 cups whole wheat flour	½ teaspoon nutmeg
1 cup mesquite meal	½ cup walnuts
(pages 71–72)	½ cup candied fruit

Preheat oven to 350 degrees F. Lightly grease two 8-inch square pans. In a large saucepan, slowly heat honey, water, and margarine until margarine is melted and honey is liquid. Mix flour, mesquite meal, baking powder, and spices in a medium bowl. Add to honey mixture and stir until well combined. Stir in nutmeats and candied fruit. Divide batter between pans. Butter fingers and pat mixture to spread evenly over pans. Bake in preheated oven for twenty to twenty-five minutes. Over-baking will make the cookies very hard. When properly baked, cookies will have a puffy look and a cakelike texture. A straw or toothpick will come out clean. Cool in pans; slice into bars. To store, place in tightly covered tins.

Mesquite Log

Makes Eight to Ten Servings

This recipe produces an extravagantly delicious dessert. I also think of it as "Election Day Cake" because I first tasted its non-mesquite prototype when a friend brought her version to a polling place where we were working. It helped us fill the long hours when no voters showed up for a non-issue election. I begged the recipe, and I think this version is better than the original.

Topping:

¼ cup butter
1 cup chopped pecans
1⅓ cups coconut
1 can Eagle Brand sweetened
   condensed milk

Cake:

3 eggs
1 cup sugar

⅓ cup mesquite meal
   (pages 71–72)
⅔ cup flour
¼ teaspoon salt
¼ teaspoon baking soda
⅓ cup water
1 teaspoon vanilla
¼ cup powdered sugar
1 tablespoon cocoa or carob
   powder

Preheat oven to 375 degrees F. Line a jelly roll pan* with foil. In a small saucepan, melt the butter and spread evenly over the foil. Layer the rest of the topping ingredients on the butter and set aside.

In a blender, beat the eggs at high speed. Add the rest of the ingredients except powdered sugar and cocoa or carob and beat. Pour evenly into pan and bake in preheated oven for twenty to twenty-five minutes.

Spread a clean, non-terry cloth tea towel on a flat surface and sprinkle with the powdered sugar and cocoa or carob. When cake is done, remove from oven and invert immediately on the towel. Carefully remove the foil. Starting with one of the long edges, roll the cake, using the tea towel to help. Cool. Slice to serve.

*The original recipe calls for a 10½ × 15½-inch pan. My jelly roll pan is 11×17, and my cake was done in the shorter baking time.

Mesquite Carrot Soup

Serves Two to Three

2 tablespoons butter
3 cups sliced carrots
½ cup chopped onion
1 large clove garlic, minced
½ cup water

1 cup mesquite broth
(pages 72–73)
1 cup whole milk
Fresh ground white pepper

In a large saucepan with a lid, melt the butter. Quickly sauté the carrot, onion, and garlic. Add the water, cover the pan, and simmer until tender. Puree carrots in blender or food processor. Return to saucepan. Add mesquite broth and milk. Season with fresh ground white pepper. Heat. Recipe is easily doubled.

Canadian Chestnut Soup

Serves Six to Eight

This makes an interesting holiday soup. If you gather mesquite pods in the summer and store them in your freezer, you will have a supply on hand when chestnuts come into season in the late autumn and winter.

2 pounds chestnuts
1 large potato, peeled and diced
2 cups chicken stock or
  bouillon
2 cups mesquite broth
(pages 72–73)
¼ cup butter

2 medium onions, chopped
6 stalks celery, chopped
1 teaspoon thyme
1 tablespoon parsley
1 cup light cream
Salt and pepper
Croutons for garnish

Place chestnuts in a large saucepan, cover with boiling water, cover saucepan, and simmer fifteen to twenty minutes. Drain and remove shells and skins. Return chestnuts to pan and add chicken stock, mesquite broth, potato, onions, celery, thyme, parsley, butter, and salt and pepper to taste. Bring soup to a boil, then lower the heat, cover, and simmer gently for about one hour or until the chestnuts are very soft. Pour the soup and its contents into a blender and puree. You will need to do this in several batches, according to the size of your blender jar. Return the soup to the saucepan and gently stir in the cream. Reheat, but do not boil. Garnish with croutons.

Mesquite Mousse
Serves Six to Eight

This is so rich that most folks will want only a small serving, but always be prepared for a few requests for seconds.

2 cups mesquite broth
  (pages 72–73)
1 can (12 ounces) evaporated
  milk
½ cup water

6 tablespoons cornstarch
2 beaten eggs
¼ cup Praline liqueur
  (optional)

Combine mesquite broth and milk in the top of a double boiler. In a small bowl or cup, combine water and cornstarch and stir until smooth. Add to mesquite mixture. Cook over boiling water for four minutes. Cover and let sit for ten minutes. Beat eggs in a bowl. Carefully add one cup of the mesquite mixture to the eggs, stirring constantly. Add egg mixture to remaining mesquite mixture and cook and stir over boiling water for four minutes. Slowly stir in the Praline liqueur. Rinse a one-quart mold with cold water. Pour mixture into mold and chill until set, about four hours. Unmold to serve.

Mesquite Instant Breakfast

Serves One

The proportions of this recipe are not terribly important. Feel free to add more of what you like, take out what you do not like, and add other ingredients not listed.

½ cup mesquite broth (pages 72–73)	1 tablespoon brewer's yeast
½ cup apple juice	½ teaspoon vanilla
½ cup buttermilk or yogurt	Sprinkle of cinnamon
1 tablespoon wheat germ	1 fruit (banana, peach, 2 apricots or figs)

Combine all ingredients in a blender and whirl until thick and smooth.

Gila Monster

Serves Six

This makes a perfect beverage for a Sunday brunch, or serve it as a substitute for dessert and after-dinner coffee. It looks especially nice in clear glass mugs or tulip-shaped stem glasses.

2½ cups cold coffee	½ cup coffee liqueur
2½ cups cold mesquite broth (pages 72–73)	Whipped cream
½ cup cold milk	Cinnamon powder

Combine all liquids in a pitcher or large bowl. Pour into glasses or cups. Top with whipped cream and a dusting of cinnamon.

Suggestion: This recipe can be varied to individual tastes. Adjust the proportions of the liquid ingredients, or substitute other liqueurs, such as creme de cacao, Praline, or brandy.

Mesquite Jelly

Makes Six to Seven Six-Ounce Glasses

This is the standard mesquite jelly recipe given out by the Pima County Agricultural Extension Service.

2½ quarts ripe mesquite pods
Water
4½ cups sugar

4 tablespoons lemon juice
1 package powdered pectin
Red food coloring (optional)

Sterilize jars and lids by boiling for fifteen minutes. Break each mesquite pod into several pieces, place in a large kettle, and add water to cover. Simmer until liquid turns yellow. Work the mass several times with a potato masher. Strain. You will need 3 cups of juice.

Place juice in a kettle or large saucepan and stir in powdered pectin. Cook and stir over high heat until mixture comes to a full boil. Add sugar and lemon juice and return to a boil. Stirring constantly, boil for one minute or until syrup comes off metal spoon in a sheet. Remove from heat. Skim off foam with metal spoon. If desired, a drop of red food coloring may be added. Pour quickly into sterilized jars or glasses. Cover at once with lids or hot paraffin.

AMARANTH

It might surprise fastidious gardeners that the "pigweed" they attack with such vengeance each summer is not only edible, but delicious. It is the close relative of what may soon become one of our newest grain staples.

Actually the word "new" only shows that history tends to repeat itself. Amaranth grain, and presumably leaves, were cultivated and eaten in Mexico 7,000 years ago. By the time of the Aztecs, thousands of hectares of amaranth were planted, and the emperor Montezuma received annual tribute of 200,000 bushels of the grain from seventeen provinces. The Aztecs not only ate the grain but used it in religious ceremonies, mixing it with the human blood of sacrificial victims and molding it into figurines.

When the Spanish arrived, Hernán Cortés decided that in the name of civilization and his Christian religion, human sacrifice had to stop. Because amaranth was so closely identified with these grisly customs, its cultivation was suppressed.

Cultivation was not eliminated, however. Amaranth survived in a few isolated pockets in Central Mexico. And farther north, on both sides of what is now the United States-Mexico border region, more than a dozen Indian tribes continued to cultivate and eat amaranth grain as well as the greens from the wild pigweeds.

Meanwhile, travelers carried the seeds to India, Asia, and Africa where they have developed into important food re-

— grain

Amaranth

sources. A recent report says that, although unlisted in agricultural statistics, leafy amaranths may be the most widely grown vegetable in the humid tropics. Among the Himalayan hill tribes, it has become a staple crop and a common grain in bread.

There are a number of reasons why amaranth can and should once again become a major plant on our own continent. First, it is extremely nutritious, with both the grain and leaves offering protein of extremely high quality as well as a wealth of vitamins and minerals (see Tables 2 and 3). The other common grains— rice, wheat and corn—lack lysine, one of the essential amino acids. Amaranth grain has lysine in abundance and is, therefore, a nutritional complement to conventional cereals. Both the grain and the leaves are high in calcium—a 3½ ounce serving of grain provides as much calcium as a glass of milk.

Table 2. Nutritional Composition of Amaranth Compared to Other Sources of Protein

Grams Per 100 Grams of Essential Amino Acids in Each Food

	Threo-nine	Valine	Leucine	Iso-Leucine	Lysine	Methio-nine	Phenyl-aline	Trypto-phan	Protein Score
Ideal Protein	11.1	13.9	19.4	11.1	15.3	9.7	16.7	2.8	100
Whole Wheat	8.9	13.5	20.4	10.0	8.7	12.3	22.9	3.3	56.9
Soy Beans	9.8	12.2	19.8	11.6	16.2	6.6	20.6	3.3	68.0
Cow's Milk	9.4	12.3	20.2	10.0	16.5	7.0	21.5	3.0	72.2
Amaranth grain	11.4	10.6	14.8	10.2	16.6	11.2	23.1	2.1	75.0

From laboratory analyses by Indigenous Foods Consultants, Inc. Ann Arbor, Michigan sponsored by Rodale R & D) in John N. Cole, *Amaranth from the past, for the future*, pp. 276–77.

Table 3. Nutritional Composition of Amaranth Compared to Other Raw Greens

Selected Nutrients in 100 Grams

	Mois-ture (%)	Pro-tein (Gr.)	Cal-cium (Mg.)	Phos-phorus (Mg.)	Iron (Mg.)	Potas-sium (Mg.)	Vit. A (I.U)	Thia-mine (Mg.)	Ribo-flavin (Mg.)	Niacin (Mg.)	Ascorbic Acid (Mg.)
Amaranth	86.9	3.5	267	67	3.9	411	6,100	.08	.16	1.4	80
Beet Greens	90.9	2.2	119	40	3.3	570	6,100	.10	.22	.4	30
Chard	91.1	2.4	88	39	3.2	550	6,500	0.06	0.17	0.5	32
Collards	85.3	4.8	250	82	1.5	450	9,300	0.16	0.31	1.7	152
Kale	87.5	4.2	179	73	2.2	378	8,900	—	—	—	125
Spinach	90.7	3.2	93	51	3.1	470	8,100	.10	.20	.6	51

From *Composition of Foods, Handbook No. 8 USDA*

A second factor making amaranth an important food for development is that the various species adapt to many environments, grow vigorously (as just about any gardener regarding them as weeds can testify), and tolerate drought well because amaranths use an especially efficient type of photosynthesis to convert soil nutrients, sunlight, and water into energy. The process is known as the C4 pathway, a very direct way of fixing carbon and building up tissues. It is used by a few other crops such as maize, sunflowers, and sugar cane, and it allows these plants to grow well at high temperatures, in bright sunlight, and under moisture stress where an ordinary plant would not thrive.

Nutritionist John Robson tried for many years to get government officials, planners, and agronomists to listen to the amaranth story and to share his enthusiasm about this ancient food. Finally, in 1972, he contacted Robert Rodale of *Organic Gardening and Farming Magazine* and Rodale Press. Rodale became intrigued with the possibilities in cultivating amaranth and threw the weight of his extensive organization into investigating just what might be done to bring amaranth up to the standards of our modern domesticated plants.

Botanists fanned out over the globe, bringing back seeds and descriptions of growth habits and use; the seeds were cataloged and stored, planted and transplanted in greenhouses and fields; the plants were photographed and tended with measured amounts of water and fertilizer and the resultant grain or leaves were weighed and measured. While the home economists in the test kitchen got to work on developing recipes for the products, packets of seeds were sent out to more than 25,000 reader-researchers contacted through Rodale's magazine. These home gardeners then reported their results to the project's coordinators. At the same time, scientists at many universities began to conduct experiments on more aspects of growing and eating the plant than the average citizen (or Aztec) could ever dream up.

What is known so far is that home gardeners like the taste of both the grain and seeds and have had pretty good luck in growing amaranth; the yield per acre is nearly at a commercially acceptable level and can certainly be improved with a little work. So far the grain is not adaptable to mechanical harvesting because the seeds tend to scatter when the ripe seedheads are brushed. Hybridization may be the solution to the latter problem, a serious obstacle to commercialization. (In Third World countries where most work is still accomplished by manual labor, mechanical harvesting is rarely an option.)

The easiest way to become involved in this exciting new culinary experiment is simply to start eating the amaranth weeds in your (or your neighbor's) yard. They usually appear in the summer and because they are ephemerals they pop up when they get moisture and grow like crazy to develop mature seeds before they die. The seeds of most wild varieties are too small to be of much use, but the leaves, if collected when young and tender, are mild-flavored and tasty. The plants are also called careless weed, bledo, and *quelité* or "greens" by the Mexican people of Sonora who gather the wild plants in abundance.

Three domesticated amaranths grown for their edible leaves are *Amaranthus tricolor* or *hinn choy*, widely used by Orientals; *A. caudatus* or Love-Lies-Bleeding, common in American flower gardens but eaten as a vegetable elsewhere; and *A. gangeticus*, known as tampala or summer spinach.

I have given only a few very traditional recipes for leaf amaranth but this vegetable can be substituted in any of the dishes described in the "Greens" section of this book.

The most widely available grain amaranth is *A. hypochondriacus* which is the heaviest yielding variety. It originated in Mexico and Central America. The very young plants are edible as greens.

You can get complete instructions for growing amaranth in your garden from your seedsman or from John N. Cole's book, *Amaranth: From the Past, For the Future,* which also offers a much more extensive discussion of the plant than I have given here.

For a list of seed companies carrying various amaranth seeds see "Sources" list at the end of the book.

Processing of Grain

Amaranth grain should be harvested when it is firm but not too dry. Two or three seed heads can be placed to dry in a gunny sack or other bag of a loose enough weave so that there is plenty of air circulation.

Cole gives instructions about how to proceed:

You can begin processing the seed when the plants are thoroughly dried. First, beat the bags with a broom or rug beater to loosen the seeds. Then, wearing stout gloves, rub the mixture through a ⅛-inch screen; this will separate the seed and chaff from the bigger pieces.

Sieve this finer part through 16-mesh window screen, a grain sieve, or a flour sifter. The end product will be fairly clean.

At this point there will be a little chaff left. You can shake the seed in a shallow pan until the chaff comes to the top then blow it off with your own breath or rig up a fan, hair dryer, or vacuum cleaner with the hose on the air vent.

Popped Amaranth

One of the Rodale reader-researchers wrote in saying: "I know now what God fed the children of Israel in the wilderness after they left Egypt—it was snow storms of popped amaranth grain. . . . The grain was as good as you said it was."

When amaranth seeds are heated they pop like tiny kernels of corn. They are a bit too small to eat like popcorn, but popped grain can be added to cereals whole or ground in a blender to make a meal or flour.

To pop amaranth seed you will need a steel wok or a deep cast iron pan. Heat the ungreased wok over medium heat, add 1 tablespoon of grain and immediately and constantly stir with a natural bristle pastry brush. As soon as the popping stops, empty the pan's contents into a bowl and start over again. If the grain does not pop, it may be because the pan is too hot, not hot enough, or the grain is too dry. In the latter case, sprinkle it with water, wait a while, and try again. One-fourth cup amaranth grain will measure a full cup when popped.

Popped Amaranth Meal

To make meal, grind popped amaranth grain a half cup at a time in an ordinary kitchen blender. (If you just cannot get it to pop, grind it like it is and substitute in the following recipes). A cup of popped amaranth will reduce to two-thirds cup when ground to meal. It can be incorporated into almost all baked goods, but remember that because amaranth grain has no gluten, it must be combined with wheat flour if you want your baked goods to rise.

It is a good idea to pop a quantity of amaranth and store it when you have time, in order to reduce the time needed for preparation of the various dishes which include popped amaranth or popped amaranth meal.

Here are two traditional recipes using amaranth greens. Amaranth leaves can also be substituted in any of the recipes in the "Greens" chapter.

West African Peanut Stew

Serves Four to Six

In much of West Africa, European-style vegetables are costly and hard to find, but leafy amaranth is usually available at a reasonable price. When I was living in Nigeria I bought small bunches of the dark green leaves from the market women who called it spinach and cooked it in delicious stews. The recipe which follows is for one such stew.

1 chicken cut into serving
   size pieces
3 cups water
3 tablespoons oil
2 medium onions, chopped
2 medium tomatoes, chopped
1 tablespoon lime juice
¼ teaspoon ground nutmeg
⅛ teaspoon ground cloves
1 teaspoon grated orange peel

½ teaspoon cayenne pepper
½ cup peanut butter
2 tablespoons cornstarch
4 cups amaranth greens

Condiments:

1 cup chopped seeded
   cucumber
1 cup chopped banana
Shredded coconut

Wash and drain very young amaranth greens. Pick off leaves, discarding woody stems. Set aside.

Place chicken in covered pan, add three cups water, and simmer until done, about thirty minutes. Reduce stock or add water to make 2 cups. In another pot, heat oil and sauté onions until limp. Add tomatoes, lime juice, nutmeg, cloves, cayenne, and orange peel and bring to a simmer. Add to chicken and stock. Cover and cook just at a simmer until chicken is tender, about fifteen minutes. Turn off heat, add amaranth, and cover.

In a small bowl, blend peanut butter with cornstarch, then add a little water to thin. Stirring, add peanut mixture to stew and cook until sauce thickens. Serve stew over hot rice and pass condiments.

Callau

Serves Four to Six

Chinese amaranth greens are traditionally used in this delicious Caribbean soup often served on the islands of Trinidad, Jamaica, and Guadaloupe. Wild amaranth or mustard leaves will do as well.

4 cups amaranth leaves
½ pound small okra
7 cups chicken stock
1 medium onion, minced
1 garlic clove, mashed
½ teaspoon dried thyme
½ cup diced ham

½ pound eggplant, peeled and chopped
½ pound fresh or frozen crabmeat (optional)
Salt and pepper
Hot pepper sauce

Using a sharp knife, shred amaranth leaves into strips about ¼ inch wide. Trim okra at stem end and at tip if necessary.

In a large saucepan, combine stock, onion, garlic, thyme, and ham. Bring to a boil over high heat; lower heat and simmer for ten minutes. Add the eggplant and cook ten minutes longer. Add okra, amaranth leaves, and crabmeat and continue simmering for ten minutes. Season with salt, pepper, and hot pepper seasoning to taste.

Amaranth Sprouts

This is a use for amaranth I never would have thought of myself. It comes from the Rodale Experimental Kitchen. If you ever made alfalfa sprouts at home, you have used the method. All you need is a jar and a piece of nylon net held on by a rubber band, or a wire tea strainer that fits tightly over the mouth of the jar.

Soak up to four tablespoons of the seed in water for about twelve hours, then drain. Rinse the sprouts by filling the jar with water and pouring it out twice a day for one day if you plan to use the sprouts in baked goods or two days if you plan to use them to add taste, texture, and nutrition to salads and sandwiches.

The flavor of these sprouts is spicy and sprout eaters enjoy their increased nutritional advantages.

The following recipes use amaranth grain.

Stuffed Zucchini

Serves Two

This is a good quick meal for two that can be doubled or tripled to serve more people.

2 fat zucchini, 6 to 7 inches
  long
1 tablespoon margarine
  or oil
4 green onions
1 tablespoon fresh parsley
½ cup popped amaranth
  grain (page 89)

¼ cup minced cooked meat
  (optional)
Salt and pepper to taste
2 tablespoons Parmesan
  cheese
2 tablespoons bread crumbs

Cut stem end from zucchini and cook in a covered frying pan or other wide shallow pan in an inch of water until just tender. Remove from water and cool. Working lengthwise, slice off top third of each zucchini and mince. Scoop out seeds from remaining portions to make "boats."

Heat margarine or oil in frying pan. Sauté sliced green onions until limp. Add parsley and sauté. Add popped amaranth and leftover meat, if desired. Season to taste with salt and pepper. Stuff zucchini boats with the mixture.

Combine Parmesan cheese and bread crumbs in a small bowl. Sprinkle on top of stuffing. Place on heat proof dish and broil until light brown on top.

O-Konomi-Yaki

Serves Four to Five

These are Japanese-style main-dish pancakes. This version does not include meat, but still it has plenty of protein. Serve it with soy sauce.

5 or 6 green onions
1 medium zucchini
1 large carrot
½ head Chinese cabbage
⅔ cup popped amaranth meal (pages 89–90)
⅔ cup whole wheat flour
⅔ cup unbleached flour
1 egg, beaten
1 tablespoon brown sugar
1 teaspoon salt
1 can (12 ounces) evaporated milk
Oil

Chop the onions fine and shred the other vegetables. Combine the flours in a large bowl and mix in the egg, sugar, salt, and milk. Fold vegetables into the batter. Bake cakes on a lightly oiled grill, turning when bottoms are brown.

Grain Amaranth Pasta

Makes About Four One-Cup Servings

Because of the complementary proteins in grain amaranth and wheat, this recipe produces a high protein pasta that requires only a light sauce—perhaps fresh tomatoes and herbs—to make a filling, nutritious meal.

1 cup popped amaranth meal   3 to 6 tablespoons water
  (pages 89–90)   Additional flour for working
1 cup all-purpose flour   the dough
2 large eggs

It is important that the popped amaranth meal be uniformly ground to a very fine texture. If your blender has not ground the grain completely, sift it through a very fine wire strainer before measuring.

Combine flours and place in a mound on a flat surface or in a wide bowl. Make a deep well in the center and crack eggs into it along with 2 tablespoons of water. Use your fingers to work these ingredients together, adding water slowly as needed. When all ingredients are mixed, knead the dough for about ten minutes. (This procedure may be accomplished in a food processor.) Cover the dough lightly and let it rest for ten minutes.

Divide the dough into four portions. On a floured board or pastry cloth roll out one portion of dough at a time into an 8 × 12-inch rectangle about ¹/₆-inch thick, trying to make as regular a shape as possible. Keep turning and flouring dough generously to keep it from sticking.

After each portion is rolled out, lay flat on a floured cloth or waxed paper. Let the pieces rest and dry, turning them once, until dough has the feel and flexibility of soft leather—five to ten minutes.

Starting with the longer edge, roll up each rectangle jelly roll style, making sure there is plenty of flour on the inner surface. Cut in ¼-inch wide strips and carefully unfurl the noodles. Dry noodles on pasta rack or cover backs of straight chairs with tea towels and drape the noodles over the chairs for up to thirty minutes.

At this point the noodles are ready to be cooked by boiling for only a few minutes in plenty of water. If you want to stop for a few hours before proceeding, put the noodles in a bowl or on a tray and cover with foil or plastic wrap until ready to cook.

Variation: Once you have gotten the hang of making home-made pasta, try substituting whole wheat flour or corn flour (not cornmeal) for the all purpose flour. The dough is a bit more difficult to work, but the flavor and nutrition are superior. A couple of tablespoons of gluten flour helps to develop springiness in the pasta.

Mexican Chili Bread
Serves Six to Eight

⅔ cup yellow corn meal
⅔ cup popped amaranth
  meal (pages 89–90)
⅔ cup flour
1 tablespoon baking powder
1 teaspoon salt
2 eggs

1 cup milk
1 cup cream-style corn
¼ cup chopped onion
¼ cup chopped green chiles
  or 1 small can (4 oz.)
¼ cup butter
½ cup shredded longhorn
  cheese

Preheat oven to 400 degrees F. Grease a 5×9-inch pan. Combine flour, baking powder, and salt in a bowl and mix well. Stir in beaten eggs, milk, and corn.

Melt butter in a skillet; add onion and sauté until onion is tender. Add onions and green chiles to batter. Stir just enough to mix. Pour half the batter into prepared loaf pan. Sprinkle with half the shredded cheese. Pour in remaining batter and top with remaining cheese. Bake in preheated oven for approximately fifty minutes, or until toothpick inserted in center comes out clean.

Vegetarian Tamale Pie

Serves Eight

The beans, tomatoes, and corn can be fresh, canned, or frozen, and proportions can vary slightly depending on what you have on hand. Although there is no meat in this dish, the ingredients complement one another so well that this dish has a high protein score.

½ cup chopped onion
½ cup chopped green pepper
3 tablespoons oil
2 cups cooked beans (tepary, pinto, or kidney)
1½ cups cooked whole kernel corn
2 cups stewed tomatoes
½ cup sliced black olives
1 teaspoon salt

2 to 3 teaspoons chili powder
¼ teaspoon garlic powder

Topping:
2½ cups cold water
1 cup cornmeal
½ cup popped amaranth meal (pages 89–90)
½ teaspoon salt
¼ cup grated cheese

Preheat oven to 375 degrees F. Sauté onion and green pepper in oil in a large pot. When tender, add beans, corn, tomatoes, olives, salt, and spices. Simmer until thick, then transfer to a large wide casserole dish.

To make topping, measure 2½ cups water into medium saucepan. Add cornmeal and amaranth flour and combine. Cook and stir over medium heat until thick. Spoon over hot vegetable mixture and sprinkle with grated cheese. Bake in preheated oven for about forty minutes.

Hi-Pro Breakfast Bars

Makes Sixteen Two-Inch Squares

If there is not time for a nourishing breakfast at your house, bake these bars over the weekend, then grab a few to eat on the way to school or work as you sail out the door each morning.

2 tablespoons butter or
   margarine
¼ cup sugar
½ teaspoon vanilla
1 tablespoon cornstarch
¾ cup cream-style cottage
   cheese
3 eggs
¼ cup frozen concentrated
   orange juice

1⅓ cups amaranth granola
   (page 98)
⅔ cup chopped walnuts
⅔ cup raisins
¼ cup flour
1 teaspoon baking powder
¼ teaspoon salt
1 teaspoon vanilla

Preheat oven to 350 degrees F. Lightly grease a 9-inch square pan. In a small bowl cream butter, sugar, and vanilla. Add cornstarch, cottage cheese, and 1 egg; beat until smooth. Set aside. In a medium bowl, beat remaining 2 eggs until frothy. Stir in orange juice concentrate, granola, walnuts, raisins, flour, baking powder, salt, and vanilla. Mix well.

Spread half of batter into prepared pan. Cover with cottage cheese mixture. Spoon remaining batter over cheese. Zigzag through batter and filling with a knife. Bake in preheated oven for forty to forty-five minutes. Cool completely before cutting into squares.

Amaranth Granola Cereal

Makes Three Quarts

3 cups popped amaranth
   (pages 89–90)
3 cups rolled oats
1 cup whole wheat flour
1 cup wheat germ
1 cup coconut
1 cup sunflower seeds

½ cup bran
1 cup raisins
½ cup water
1 cup oil
1 cup honey
1 tablespoon vanilla

Preheat oven to 250 degrees F. Combine all dry ingredients except raisins in a large bowl. Combine wet ingredients in a small saucepan and heat over low heat until honey is liquid. Pour over dry ingredients, mixing well. Spread in a large shallow baking pan and bake in preheated oven for one hour. Occasionally stir the mixture so that the toasted layer on the bottom does not become too brown. When granola is an even golden brown, remove from oven and mix in the raisins. Cool. Store in airtight cans or jars.

Raisin Nut Bread

Makes One Loaf

This bread is especially good at breakfast time, toasted or made into French toast.

1 cup popped amaranth meal
   (pages 89–90)
2 cups whole wheat flour
¼ cup toasted wheat germ
2 teaspoons baking powder
1¼ teaspoons soda

½ teaspoon salt
1½ cups buttermilk
½ cup honey
¼ cup vegetable oil
½ cup raisins
½ cup chopped nuts

Preheat oven to 325 degrees F. Grease a 5 × 9-inch loaf pan.

In a large bowl combine the dry ingredients. In another bowl, combine the buttermilk, honey, and oil. Add wet mixture all at once to flour mixture, stirring quickly just to moisten. Stir in the raisins and nuts, using as few strokes as possible.

Pour batter into greased loaf pan and bake for one hour and fifteen minutes in preheated oven. (A toothpick inserted in the middle of the loaf should come out clean.) Cool for ten minutes before removing bread from pan. Cool loaf completely before slicing.

Chewy Amaranth Brownies
Makes Twenty Bars

A very few forward-looking companies have begun to include amaranth grain in their commercial products. Health Valley Natural Foods has developed this recipe for their amaranth cereal. Homemade amaranth granola (page 98) can be substituted.

2 eggs
¾ cup honey
½ cup vegetable oil
2 cups amaranth cereal or
    granola

½ cup whole wheat flour
⅓ cup carob powder
    or cocoa
½ teaspoon baking soda
1 teaspoon cream of tartar
½ cup slivered almonds

Beat together eggs, honey, and oil in a large bowl. Add cereal and allow to stand for thirty minutes.

Preheat oven to 350 degrees F. Lightly grease an 8 × 12-inch baking pan. Sift together flour, carob powder or cocoa, soda, and cream of tartar. Add to soaked cereal mixture, then stir in almonds. Spread batter evenly into prepared baking pan and bake in preheated oven for twenty-five minutes. Cool five minutes; cut into squares.

Grandma's Honey Cookies

Makes Four Dozen Cookies

This recipe makes a very wholesome-tasting cookie, with more protein than a cookie really ought to have.

⅔ cup popped amaranth
    meal (pages 89—90)
1⅓ cups whole wheat flour
1 teaspoon baking powder
½ teaspoon baking soda
½ teaspoon nutmeg
2 tablespoons powdered milk
½ cup butter

½ cup honey
1 tablespoon grated lemon or
    orange rind
1 tablespoon vanilla
1 egg
½ cup raisins, chopped
½ cup carob or chocolate
    chips

Preheat oven to 375 degrees F. Combine dry ingredients in a large bowl. Using a pastry blender or two knives, cut in butter until mixture resembles corn meal. In a medium bowl, beat honey, rind, vanilla and egg until well combined; add to flour. (In food processor fitted with a steel blade, combine flours, cut butter into 4 pieces, bury butter pieces in flour and process. Add wet ingredients and process.)

Stir in raisins and carob or chocolate chips. Drop by rounded teaspoons on ungreased cookie sheets. Flatten slightly with a fork dipped in sugar. Bake ten minutes in preheated oven.

Alegria

Makes Sixteen Two-Inch Squares

This is the classic Mexican candy for which amaranth grain is widely used in Mexico.

4 teaspoons honey
2 teaspoons molasses
1 tablespoon butter

1 cup popped amaranth
  seeds (page 89)

Grease an 8-inch square pan. In a saucepan, combine honey, molasses, and butter. Cook over medium heat, stirring constantly to prevent burning, until mixture becomes golden, about six minutes. Spread the popped amaranth in prepared pan. Pour the syrup over it and mix well. Pat the mixture evenly into the pan. When cool cut in squares or bars.

Energy Master Mix

Although this basic mix can be used at any time to make the recipes below, it is especially handy to take on camping trips when increased physical activity makes it important to get good nutrition.

1 cup popped amaranth meal
  (pages 89–90)
1 cup whole wheat flour
2 cups all purpose flour
½ cup soy flour
¼ cup wheat germ

2½ tablespoons baking
  powder
1¼ teaspoons salt
⅔ cup dry milk powder
¼ cup sugar
¾ cup vegetable oil

Thoroughly blend together all ingredients and package airtight in plastic bags or containers. Refrigerate until needed.

Trailside Dumplings

Serves Six

1 cup Energy Master Mix   ⅓ cup water
  (page 101)   1 teaspoon favorite herb
1 egg

Heat stew or soup of your choice to boiling in a pot with a tight-fitting lid. Combine Energy Master Mix, egg, water, and herb in a medium bowl. Drop batter by heaping tablespoons on top of simmering liquid. Cover and cook for fifteen minutes. *Do not lift the lid.* Dumplings should be dry on top and cooked through.

Energy Pancakes

Makes Nine to Ten Pancakes

1 cup Energy Master Mix   ½ cup water
  (page 101)   Oil or margarine
1 egg

In a small bowl combine Energy Master Mix, egg, and water and mix lightly. Mixture will be lumpy. Heat oil or margarine in large heavy frying pan. Pour or spoon about ¼ cup batter into pan for each pancake, spreading it into a 4-inch circle. Cook until the bubbles begin to break on the top and the bottoms are nicely browned. Flip and brown other side. Serve with butter, honey, syrup, or whatever delicious berries you have managed to forage.

Dutch Oven Biscuits

You will never remember these directions, so you had better photocopy this page and stick it in your camping gear. For baking purposes you will need an old-fashioned dutch oven (with legs and a ridge around the rim of the lid).

Build a fire using hard wood. When you have coals, move some to the side, place the dutch oven on them, and spread a shovelful of coals evenly on the lid.

While the oven is heating, combine 2 cups of Energy Master Mix (page 101) with ½ cup water, or a little more if necessary, to make a soft dough. Knead a few times and separate and shape dough into twelve or fourteen biscuits. Place them on a plate or piece of foil.

Remove the dutch oven from the fire, minus the lid which should continue to heat, and put a tablespoon of fat in it. The oven should be warm enough to melt the grease slowly; if it sizzles the oven is too hot. Let it cool a bit as you smear the grease around.

Then arrange the biscuits, crowding them so that the sides touch. Put a shovelful of small coals on a flat spot and set the pot on it. Put the lid on the pot and arrange a shovelful of coals on the lid. (You will want more heat on top than on the bottom. A common mistake is to get too many coals under the pot and not enough on top.)

In five minutes check the biscuits, lifting the lid with a sturdy stick or pliers. If the biscuits are rising and starting to brown they are just right. If the bottoms are browning too fast, take the pot off the coals. If the tops are too brown, take the lid off for a minute. In a couple more minutes rotate the pot one quarter turn and the lid one quarter turn to even out hot spots. The biscuits should be done in about fifteen minutes from the time they went in the oven.

(I did not know a thing about dutch oven cookery until I read *Chuck Wagon Cookin'* by Stella Hughes, a book I recommend to all campers.)

Wild Greens

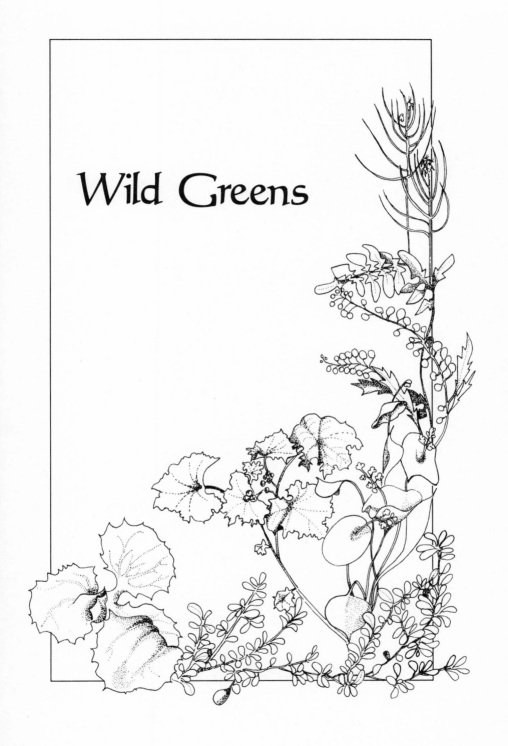

When I first began studying wild plants nearly fifteen years ago, I despaired of ever being able to tell one green, leafy plant from another. Now as I walk along city streets or desert trails, I have a much different relationship to the plants I pass, whether they are growing up through the sidewalk cracks or hiding under rocks or making an untidy mess in my own front yard. I am on a first name basis with many of the plants, and although I may not always pick them up and take them home for dinner, I view them not as obnoxious invaders or anonymous ground covers, but as living things with which I have at least the possibility of beneficial interaction. I am a person who likes to know my neighbors, be they people or plants.

And the interaction is beneficial—at least on my side. Wild greens are so bursting with vitamins and minerals that they leave our common salad green, iceberg lettuce, looking pallid by comparison. All greens provide calcium, iron, carotene (pre-vitamin A), riboflavin, folic acid, and vitamin C. One example of the superior vitamin content of wild greens is purslane which contains four times as much vitamin C as head lettuce, seven times as much calcium, and five times as much iron.

Wild greens usually appear with the early spring and late summer rains. Most of them are ephemerals so, especially in the hot areas, they go through their growth cycle very quickly and are at the fresh and tender stage for only a brief time. Older, flowering greens are most often bitter.

Take care when gathering greens from a spot other than your own yard. Plants near roadways may contain toxins from car exhaust. Greens found near agricultural fields may have been sprayed with pesticides; check with the nearest farmer to make sure the greens are untainted.

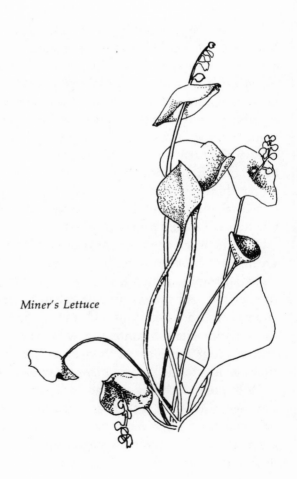

Miner's Lettuce

MINER'S LETTUCE

Miner's lettuce (*Montia perfoliata*) is one of the most delicate and desirable of the wild greens. During the California Gold Rush, it was relished by the forty-niners who quickly became weary of their diet of meat and flapjacks. In the hot deserts, miner's lettuce is available only in the very early spring, but in the cool mountains it tends to stay fresh longer. It grows in damp places along creeks. To find it you have to bend down and search under overhanging rocks and dense bushes.

Miner's lettuce has two kinds of leaves: heart-shaped and disk-shaped, which grow completely around the stem. Unlike the blossoms of other greens, the small white flowers of miner's lettuce do not seem to signal bitterness in the leaves.

Although it can be cooked, cooking this most delicate of greens seems a travesty. The best way to eat it is to sit in the middle of a patch and start munching. However, if you insist on dealing with it in a more civilized manner, be advised that the leaves wilt extremely fast in the heat of a backpack. If you are hiking to a known patch of miner's lettuce with the intent of picking for home use, take along a wide-mouth thermos or a similar contrivance to protect your harvest.

The lightest sprinkling of vinaigrette is all the dressing you will need on your salad as the leaves taste slightly tangy all by themselves.

MONKEY FLOWER

Monkey flower (*Mimulus guttatus*) is another early spring green that grows either in the middle of streams or on the banks where the ground is damp. The leaves are about the size of a quarter, round or slightly oval, with toothed edges and sometimes a very slightly hairy surface. They look remarkably like the common houseplant called Creeping Charley. The flowers resemble tiny yellow snapdragons but by the time those appear the plant will be much too bitter to eat.

Like miner's lettuce, monkey flower is best picked very young and fresh and eaten raw with a light dressing.

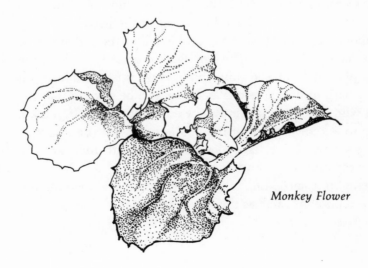

Monkey Flower

PEPPER GRASS

Pepper grass (*Lepidium spp.*) is common throughout the West. The various species range from only a few inches in height to a shrubby variety that grows a meter high. You will find it in the spring along roadsides, in fields, pastures, waste places, mesas, washes, river bottoms, and maybe your own backyard. The distinguishing feature is the tiny seed pods which have a sharp and pleasant bite. I have read that some people cook the whole plant, but I find the stems too woody for that. I prefer to strip off the seed pods and combine them in salad dressings or sprinkle them over a salad of sliced cucumbers and tomatoes.

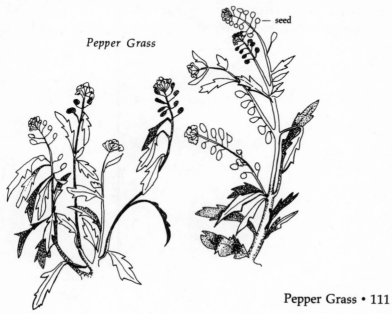

— seed

Pepper Grass

WILD MUSTARD

The mustard family includes many leafy plants both wild and cultivated. *Sisymbrium Irio* and *S. officianale* are two of the tastiest specimens if picked young. *S. Irio* has smooth, lobed leaves; the leaves of *S. officianale* are somewhat hairy. The tender, spicy leaves of wild mustards appear in the deserts as early as January if the weather is wet. They are often so abundant they become a pest. You can deal with them effectively and economically by using them in the following recipes. (Wild mustards are among the most widely recognized edible plants; if these two varieties do not occur in your area, ask around at your closest agricultural extension office or college in the spring and you will probably find somebody happy to point out your local edibles.)

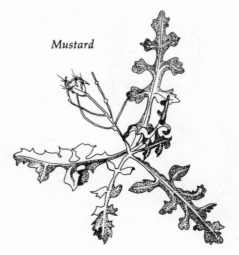

Mustard

The small yellow flowers are also edible with a sharp horse-radish-like bite to them. But try one first before using them extensively to see if they suit your taste.

Wild Greens Soup

Serves Four

This soup is an intense yet soft green. I often use it as the first course for a dinner party. Mustard or amaranth greens may be used.

8 cups greens	2 cups chicken stock or
2 green onions	bouillon
1 small clove garlic	1¼ cups milk
1 tablespoon butter	1 lemon
2 tablespoons flour	

Reserve ½ cup greens. Plunge remaining greens in boiling water for five minutes. Drain and press out excess water. Melt butter in large heavy saucepan over low heat; add chopped green onions and sauté. When onions are limp, add flour and stir. Stirring constantly, slowly add 1 cup of water or stock and cook until smooth. Transfer sauce and cooked, drained greens to container of blender and puree. Return to saucepan. Add remaining stock and milk and blend.

Slice 4 thin slices of lemon from center of fruit. Reserve. Squeeze one of remaining halves to produce 1 tablespoon of juice and add to soup. Finely chop reserved ½ cup of greens.

To serve, dish soup into bowls. Float lemon slices on soup, topped with a tiny pile of spicy chopped leaves.

Chinese Mustard Green Soup

Serves Four

This soup is traditionally made with Chinese mustard greens but the small wild variety works just as well. Chinese amaranth greens can also be used.

¼ pound lean pork
1 tablespoon soy sauce
2 teaspoons sesame oil
1 teaspoon oyster sauce
½ cup chicken broth
4 cups water

1 cup shredded fresh mustard greens
2 green onions, chopped (including most of green tops)

With a sharp knife, slice pork very thin; shred into matchstick-size pieces. Combine meat in a bowl with soy sauce, oyster sauce, and 1 teaspoon of the sesame oil. Marinate fifteen minutes. Meanwhile, combine chicken broth and water in medium saucepan. Bring to a boil, then reduce heat. Add mustard greens and pork with its marinade. Cook gently for about seven minutes. Stir in remaining sesame oil and green onion.

Green Mayonnaise

Makes Three-and-a-Half Cups

This can be used as a dip for vegetables or served in a bowl alongside a plate of fresh sliced tomatoes.

1 cup thick yogurt
½ cup mustard leaves and flowers
1 cup spinach leaves
¼ cup fresh chopped parsley

3 green onions, chopped
½ teaspoon horseradish
1 cup mayonnaise
Lemon juice
Salt

If yogurt is not thick, line a colander with cheesecloth and drain yogurt until consistency of sour cream. Chop mustard and spinach leaves coarsely. Bring a large pot of water to a boil and drop in spinach and mustard for a few seconds. Drain, rinse with cold water and drain again. Add yogurt, spinach and mustard leaves, parsley, chopped green onions, and horseradish to blender jar or food processor bowl. Blend just to mix. In a medium bowl combine mayonnaise and blended mixture. Add lemon juice and salt to taste.

Fresh Mustard Salad

Serves Six to Eight

The secret to this delicious combination is to pick the mustard leaves when they are young and fresh, before any bitterness is evident.

1 cup mustard leaves	½ bunch romaine
1 head bibb lettuce	1 cup broken walnut meats

Break up lettuce leaves and toss with mustard leaves and walnuts. Immediately before serving dress with Walnut Vinaigrette.

Walnut Vinaigrette:

3 tablespoons walnut oil	Dash salt
½ cup olive, vegetable, or safflower oil	1 clove crushed garlic or garlic juice
¼ cup red wine vinegar	Fresh ground pepper
2 tablespoons lemon juice	

Combine oils in a small bowl. Wisk in vinegar, lemon juice, garlic, salt, and pepper. Or put all ingredients in a jar, cover tightly, and shake vigorously.

WATERCRESS

This is one of the most widespread and widely recognized wild greens. It is found growing in streams and springs even during the winter if it is not too cold.

Watercress was known in ancient Greek and Roman times and various writers disagreed about whether it was a delicious herb or a harmful pest.

The debate continues today in our own country. When I was doing research for my first cookbook, I spent an afternoon with a Havasupai woman deep in Supai Canyon at one end of the Grand Canyon. She pointed out many plants, but back in my own camp that night I realized she had not mentioned the watercress that grows so abundantly there. The next day I asked her about it.

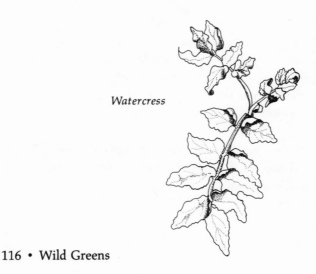

Watercress

"That's food for horses," was her reply.

"But the white people eat it," I prodded. "They even sell it in the grocery stores."

"Well, the Havasupais think it is food for horses," she said with a shake of her head and that was the end of the discussion.

We usually think of watercress simply as an ingredient in salads but the possibilities for its use are much more extensive as you can see in the following recipes.

Watercress Salad
Serves Six to Eight

This version of the recipe calls for watercress and spinach, but most spring or summer wild greens go well in this sprightly salad.

3 cups watercress
1 cup wild greens or spinach
10 large white mushrooms

1 medium red or green bell
    pepper
1 small apple

Rinse greens well in large pan of water. Remove tough stems and any discolored leaves. Slice mushrooms, bell pepper, and apple. Refrigerate until serving, then toss with your favorite dressing or use the recipe below.

Mellow Vinaigrette:

⅓ cup olive oil
⅓ cup light vegetable oil
⅓ cup wine vinegar
2 tablespoons tomato juice

1 teaspoon Dijon mustard
½ teaspoon sugar
½ teaspoon salt
Grating of fresh pepper

Combine oils in a small bowl. Wisk in vinegar, tomato juice, mustard, and seasonings. Or put all ingredients in a jar, cover tightly, and shake vigorously.

Watercress Salad Dressing

Makes About Two-and-a-Half Cups

This is good over fresh sliced cucumbers or cold boiled shrimp.

2 cups packed watercress
2 tablespoons lemon juice
1 tablespoon wine vinegar
⅛ teaspoon tarragon

½ cup olive oil
1 teaspoon salt
4 or 5 gratings of fresh
  pepper

Wash and pick over watercress for any tough or discolored bits. Pat dry with clean tea towel. In a food processor chop the watercress first, then add remaining ingredients. If using a blender, combine liquid ingredients first, then add watercress and blend until finely chopped.

Oriental Watercress

Makes Two to Three Servings

3 tablespoons peanut or
  light vegetable oil
  (no substitutes)
2 thin slices ginger root,
  chopped fine

3 green onions, chopped
1 carrot, sliced to pieces the
  size of a matchstick
2 cups watercress
Soy sauce

Heat oil in wok or large frying pan. Add ginger root and green onion and sauté one minute. Remove with slotted spoon and reserve. Sauté carrot until tender. Add watercress, ginger, and onion and toss until watercress is slightly wilted. Serve with soy sauce to taste.

Watercress Sandwiches

Makes Fifty-Six Tea Sandwiches

If you are hankering for something really upperclass for your party, but the contents of your wallet will not buy caviar, try watercress sandwiches. They are quite tasty and not at all difficult or costly to prepare. The following recipe is adapted from Gourmet Magazine.

3 cups watercress
1 cup (2 sticks) butter
2 tablespoons fresh parsley
   leaves, minced
1 tablespoon fresh tarragon,
   minced, or 1 teaspoon
   dried tarragon

1 teaspoon Dijon mustard
1 teaspoon Worcestershire
   sauce
1 teaspoon fresh lemon juice
Salt and pepper
28 slices very thin
   homemade style bread

Bring a large pot of water to a boil over high heat. Take half the watercress, plunge it into boiling water for one minute, drain, then press it dry. When cool enough to handle, chop fine. In a large bowl, cream the butter until light, blend in cooked watercress, parsley, tarragon, mustard, Worcestershire sauce, lemon juice, and salt and pepper to taste. Let the butter stand in a cool place for about one hour.

Meanwhile, trim the crusts from the bread and roll each slice as thin as possible with a rolling pin. Spread each slice with the herb butter and arrange four sprigs of the reserved watercress on each slice, two pointing to the left and two to the right, so that the leaves will protrude from each end when the bread is rolled. Beginning with the edge nearest you, roll up the sandwiches. Arrange on a baking sheet, seam side down, and chill, covered for one hour.

To serve, halve each roll crosswise and arrange rolls in concentric circles like a flower with rows of petals. A cherry tomato, a tomato peel rose, or a carved radish in the very center of the plate adds a nice touch of color.

Watercress Pineapple Snow

Makes One-and-a-Half Quarts

I have often considered putting together a dinner party so classy that we would pause mid-meal to "refresh our palates" with a sorbet. If I ever get around to arranging such an occasion, I will use this recipe I found in the Dallas Times-Herald.

1½ cups granulated sugar
1 cup water
⅓ cup watercress leaves
Pulp of 2 large or 3 small
  limes

2½ cups chopped fresh
  pineapple (about 1
  pineapple)
Watercress sprigs

Combine sugar and water in a medium saucepan over medium heat. Stir to dissolve sugar. Remove from heat. Cool.

Pick watercress leaves off of stalks and measure. Combine with lime pulp and pineapple in a food processor container. Puree until smooth. Combine with cooled sugar syrup. Pour into cannister of an ice cream maker and process according to manufacturer's directions.

To serve, spoon into pretty glasses and garnish each with a watercress sprig.

TUMBLEWEED

Tumbleweeds seem as at home on the range as cowboys and longhorns and other trappings of the Old West. Actually tumbleweeds, also called Russian thistle (*Salsola Kali*), were first introduced into the United States in 1873 mixed with flaxseed obtained from Eurasia.

Because of their ability to use a little water to great advantage and to grow in waste places, the plant spread quickly over the West and is found widely in disturbed soils in low to medium elevations.

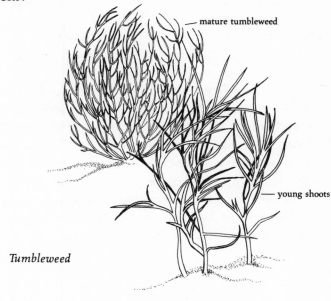

— mature tumbleweed

— young shoots

Tumbleweed

Of all the plants to which I have introduced people, tumbleweed is approached the most gingerly and embraced the most enthusiastically. The sprouts appear after spring and summer rains and grow quickly. They must be picked when they are two or three inches tall.

Steamed Tumbleweed Sprouts

Gather sprouts and wash well, pinching off and discarding the roots and any sprouts which have matured to the point of feeling prickly. Steam for five to ten minutes. Toss with butter and lemon juice.

Tumbleweed Casserole
Serves Six to Eight

2 cups tumbleweed sprouts	1 cup shredded longhorn
4 eggs	cheese
2 cups creamed cottage cheese	¼ teaspoon hot pepper sauce
1 can (8 ounces) whole-	Salt and pepper
kernel corn	¼ cup butter
⅓ cup chopped green onion	½ cup breadcrumps

Grease an 11×7-inch ovenproof dish or similar round casserole. Wash and sort tumbleweed sprouts, discarding roots and any sprouts which have matured to the point of feeling prickly. Chop coarsely. Place tumbleweed sprouts in prepared dish. Combine eggs and cottage cheese in large bowl and mix well. Add drained corn, green onion, shredded cheese, hot pepper sauce, salt, and pepper. Pour over the tumbleweed sprouts. Melt the butter over low heat and combine with the bread crumbs. Sprinkle over top of casserole. Bake at 350 degrees F. for forty-five minutes.

Jellied Tumbleweed Salad

Serves Twelve to Fourteen

Gelatin salads are a Texas tradition and so are tumbleweeds, but this is probably the first time anybody thought of putting the two together.

1 cup tightly packed
   tumbleweed sprouts
2 envelopes unflavored gelatin
½ cup sugar
1 teaspoon salt
1½ cups boiling water
1½ cups cold water
⅓ cup vinegar

⅓ cup lemon juice
½ cup finely shredded
   cabbage
½ cup chopped celery
½ cup shredded carrots
¼ cup chopped green bell
   pepper

Wash and sort tumbleweed sprouts, discarding roots and any sprouts which have matured to the point of feeling prickly. Chop fine. Set aside.

Mix gelatin, sugar, and salt in a large bowl. Add boiling water and stir until gelatin dissolves. Add cold water, vinegar, and lemon juice. Chill until partially set. Add chopped tumbleweed sprouts, celery, carrots, and green bell pepper and mix. Rinse a seven-cup mold with cold water. Pour in the gelatin and vegetable mixture; chill for four hours or until set. Unmold on lettuce leaves.

Tumbleweed Fritata

Serves Two

Great for brunch or a light supper. If you have a food processor, use it to slice the potatoes and chop the onion.

1 cup tumbleweed sprouts	1 onion, chopped
3 tablespoons butter or	3 eggs
margarine	2 tablespoons water
2 potatoes, sliced	Salt and pepper

Wash and sort tumbleweed sprouts, discarding roots and any sprouts which have matured to the point of feeling prickly. Chop and set aside. Melt the butter in a large skillet. Sauté chopped onion until limp. Add sliced potatoes and chopped tumbleweed, layering evenly over bottom of skillet. Turn heat to low, cover skillet, and sauté potatoes until almost soft, stirring and turning occasionally. Beat eggs and add water, salt, and pepper to taste. Pour over vegetables and continue cooking on low, shaking pan occasionally and lifting vegetables with a spatula so egg can run underneath. Cook until eggs are set.

POVERTY WEED

Poverty weed (*Monolepsis nuttalliana*) came upon its name because so many people have resorted to eating it in times of want. It is unfortunate that the name has stuck, because it makes the plant seem less desirable than its delicate flavor would indicate. Perhaps the Spanish term *patota*, or the Papago name *opon*, which means "lacy," are better names.

The plant comes up with the first winter rains and is found as early as February in low spots, along roadsides and barren areas on mesas, and in places where the soil tends to be alkaline. It grows low to the ground and sometimes in dense thick patches. It has been found as high as 7,500 feet, but usually below 3,000 feet.

It can be prepared by boiling or steaming, or used in any of these recipes for wild greens.

Poverty Weed

CHEESE WEED

Cheese weed (*Malva parviflora, M. neglecta*) occurs throughout the West from spring through early fall. It is a native of the Old World which somehow made its way to these shores many years ago. The shape of the leaves is somewhat like that of geranium leaves although smaller, and the fruits are shaped like little round cheeses. The greens can be eaten raw but because of their slight hairiness are better when steamed and cooked into one of the dishes for wild greens at the end of this section.

The fruits make good additions to salads as a substitute for capers if they are soaked overnight in a strong salt solution, then pickled with any ordinary pickling solution. Let them cure for three months before using.

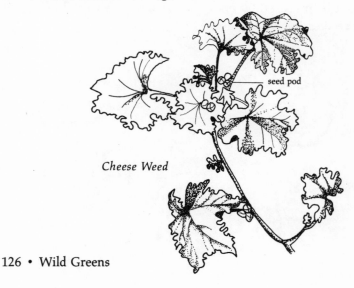

Cheese Weed

PURSLANE

Purslane (*Portulaca* spp. and *Trianthema portulacastrum*) is a common garden weed and is also found in fields where there is irrigation, or after rains. The true portulacas are the most desirable and are often sold in the late summer in southwestern grocery stores under the name *verdolagas*.

Both plants grow low to the ground, have pinkish, fleshy stems, and succulent leaves. *Trianthema* is not as good raw as *Portulaca*.

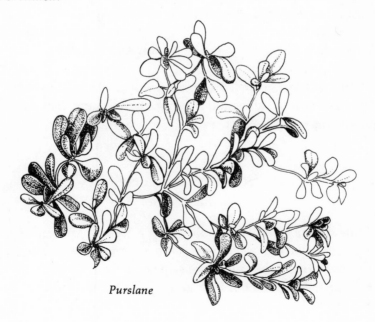

Purslane

The traditional Mexican way to eat purslane is chopped and mixed with tomatoes and onions, doused with vinegar and oil, and topped with crumbly white cheese. Mexican home economist Rosa Maria de Valdivia took me to a market outside of Mexico City where the vegetable saleswomen had prepared huge bowls of the salad that shoppers could buy in bulk and carry home with them.

Another traditional recipe is to toss the cut-up greens with onions fried in bacon grease. Try chopped and steamed purslane also in the following recipes which can be used to put any wild green in shape for the dinner table.

Dressed-Up Greens

Serves Four to Six

Almost any wild green that is good cooked is even better in this recipe.

6 cups greens (or 3 cups if using tumbleweed sprouts)	2 cloves garlic, minced
	3 tablespoons sliced almonds
1 teaspoon salt	½ cup sliced green olives
¼ cup olive oil	1 tablespoon capers

Wash and sort greens. Steam until wilted over boiling water. Chop. Heat oil in skillet and stir in garlic and nuts. Sauté until golden. Add olives, capers, and greens. Serve warm.

Squares of Green

Serves Eight to Ten

This is one of my all-time favorite recipes for brunches, christening lunches, wedding receptions, and special dinner parties. Mustard, amaranth, or poverty weed work equally well. If you do not have enough wild greens, use some spinach.

5 cups greens
3 tablespoons butter or
    margarine
1 small onion, chopped
¼ pound mushrooms, sliced
4 eggs
¼ cup fine dry bread crumbs

1 can condensed cream of
    mushroom soup
¼ cup grated Parmesan
    cheese
¼ teaspoon basil
⅛ teaspoon pepper

Grease a 9-inch square baking pan. Preheat oven to 325 degrees F. Plunge greens into boiling water for one minute, drain, and chop. Place in wire strainer and press out all liquid. (This is nutritious and can be saved to add to soups or gravies.)

Melt butter in a frying pan over medium heat. Add the onion and mushrooms and sauté until onion is limp. In a bowl, beat the eggs with a fork, then beat in crumbs, mushroom soup, half of the cheese, basil, pepper to taste, spinach, and onion mixture.

Turn into prepared baking pan and sprinkle with the remaining cheese. Bake uncovered in preheated oven for thirty-five minutes or until set when touched lightly. Cool. Cut into squares.

Serve at room temperature or reheat for ten to twelve minutes.

Down Home Greens

Serves Two to Four

Caterer and gourmet cook Stephanie Daniel grew up in a Southern California household where greens-picking was a family tradition. This is one of the family recipes for greens.

5 to 6 cups raw wild greens
½ cup chopped, chilled
    tomatoes

¼ cup chopped onion
White vinegar
Salt and pepper

Boil or steam the greens until tender. Cool and mix with tomatoes and onions. Add vinegar, salt, and pepper to taste.

Savory Pastries

Makes Eight Pastries

¾ cup chopped cooked greens
½ cup grated Parmesan
   cheese
2 green onions, chopped

1 egg, beaten
1 tube of refrigerated
   crescent roll dough

Preheat oven to 400 degrees F. Press cooked greens into a sieve with the back of a spoon to remove all excess liquid. Combine greens with the cheese, onions and about half of the beaten egg.

Carefully unroll dough and separate into triangles. Gently stretch each triangle so that it is more or less equilateral. To fill, place a triangle of dough in front of you so that it is pointing away from you. Place ⅛ of the filling in the middle of the triangle then bring both the right and left points to the top point. Press seams together to contain filling. Transfer to an ungreased cookie sheet. Brush top of pastries with remaining beaten egg. Bake in preheated oven until well-browned on top. May be served whole or cut into sections for hors d'oeuvres. Best when hot.

Greens and Yogurt Salad

Serves Six

1 clove garlic
1 medium onion
2 to 3 tablespoons water
4 cups wild greens
2 cups plain yogurt
½ cup chopped pecans
1 tablespoon salad oil

2 tablespoons lemon juice
2 teaspoons crumbled dried
   mint or 2 tablespoons
   fresh mint
1½ teaspoons salt
½ teaspoon pepper

Mince garlic and thinly slice onion. In a covered saucepan cook onion and garlic in 2 to 3 tablespoons water over medium heat for about three minutes or until onion is tender. Gradually add greens to saucepan, stirring frequently until greens are just wilted. Drain and cool. In a bowl combine spinach mixture, yogurt, and other ingredients, tossing gently until well-coated. Cover and refrigerate for at least three hours.

Greens in Artichoke Bottoms

Sometimes elegance is more important than budget watching, and this recipe is just perfect for those special occasions.

6 cups greens
1 package (8 ounces) cream cheese
1 medium onion, finely chopped
½ cup mayonnaise
1 egg
1 teaspoon basil

1 teaspoon salt
½ teaspoon pepper
2 cans artichoke bottoms (10 to 14 artichokes)
3 tablespoons grated Parmesan cheese
1 tablespoon paprika

Wash and sort greens. Steam greens over boiling water until just wilted. When cool, chop. Combine cream cheese, chopped onion, mayonnaise, egg, basil, salt, and pepper in a bowl. Stir in greens. Rinse and drain artichoke bottoms, then spoon cheese mixture into the hollows. Sprinkle with Parmesan and paprika. Broil until tops are bubbly.

Wild Greens Soufflé

Serves Two to Three

Use any wild greens or a mixture in this soufflé.

3 tablespoons butter	4 eggs separated
3 tablespoons flour	¼ teaspoon nutmeg
1 cup light cream or milk	Salt and pepper
1 cup grated Swiss cheese	Grated Parmesan cheese
1 cup cooked wild greens	

Preheat oven to 325 degrees F. Butter a two-quart soufflé dish and dust with Parmesan cheese.

Heat the butter in a saucepan; stir in the flour and cook, continuing to stir constantly for about two minutes. Gradually add the cream, using a wire whisk to produce a smooth thick sauce. Season with salt, pepper, and nutmeg. Reduce heat and stir in the greens and the Swiss cheese. Allow the sauce to cool.

Meanwhile, separate the eggs and beat the yolks until thick and add to cream sauce, first pouring a bit of the sauce into the eggs to heat them up. Beat the egg whites until stiff but not dry. Fold half of the egg whites into the cream sauce until well combined. Lightly fold the second half of the egg whites into the mixture.

Turn soufflé mixture into the prepared soufflé dish. Using a spatula, cut a ring around the top of the soufflé about 1 inch in from the rim of the dish; this will help it puff nicely. Bake in preheated oven for about forty minutes.

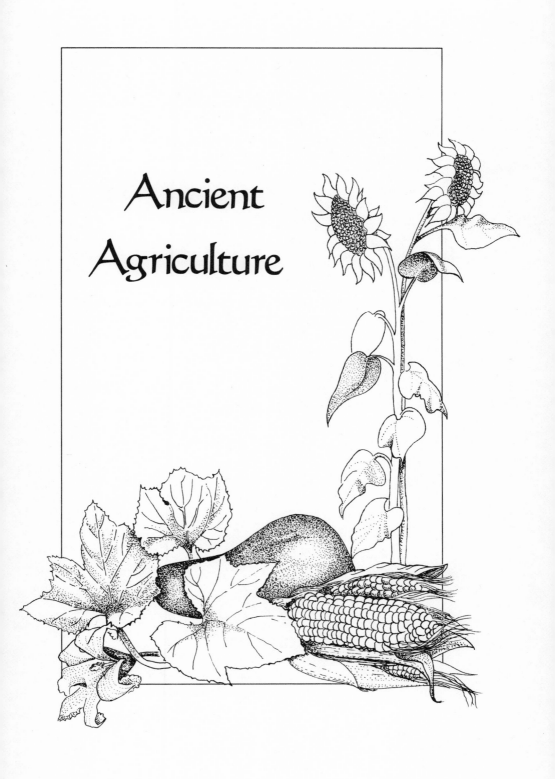

Ancient
Agriculture

TEPARY BEANS

The United States is currently undergoing a revival of dried bean consciousness. Magazines and newspaper food sections vie to bring us recipes for pink beans, white beans, red beans, and black beans; large limas, baby limas, pintos, and garbanzos.

The typical consumer may be overwhelmed when presented with such diversity, but it takes a real insider to know what is left out of these commercially contrived lists. Tepary beans, both venerable and promising, have gotten short shrift.

Wild and domesticated teparies (*Phaseolus acutifolius*) have been around the American hemisphere for 5,000 years. Many southwestern Indian tribes grew the beans, but none relied on them or relished them more than the O'odham of Arizona. It is not hard to understand why the O'odham were called the Bean People when we realize that as late as 1940 the average O'odham consumed about three-quarters of a pound of beans daily. Teparies even figure in their creation myth. When these desert Indians get together to recount their ancient stories, the children learn how the Milky Way was formed of white tepary beans untold centuries ago.

Anglo-American farmers had a brief flirtation with tepary farming beginning around 1914 when the bean was introduced commercially into California. Other farmers in Arizona and New Mexico began cultivating the little bean when they heard

Tepary Beans

that teparies were a nutritious crop adapted over centuries to dryland farming. In wet years, teparies achieved or surpassed the average bean yield without irrigation and in drought years teparies still produced a small crop when other crops failed completely.

That was before mass marketing and new-product introduction techniques had been developed to their present levels, however, and though the beans grew in the field, they died in the marketplace. Farmers who could not sell them did not want to grow them. Then, before they really had a chance to catch on, gasoline-powered engines made it possible for farmers to suck up groundwater to irrigate their dry fields. Drought-hardiness became an irrelevant issue, and when the farmers grew beans, they planted new hybrids instead.

Small-scale Mexican and Indian farmers began to turn to the hybrids as well, but also kept small plots of teparies. The older farmers, particularly, were reluctant to give up something that had been so important to their people.

The Indians' preference for tepary beans was based on more than emotional factors. I once talked to an elderly Papago who said that in the past tepary beans had been a particularly good traveling food, because human beings could be well-nourished by eating these beans just once a day, whereas they would require two servings of another kind of bean.

Since then, scientific analyses have shown us that teparies rank slightly higher than most other beans in protein and niacin, and quite a lot higher in calcium (important for people who do not use dairy products). (See Tables 4 and 5.)

With today's dwindling water resources, teparies are again attracting attention from commercial agriculture. Unfortunately, many of the genetic strains and color variations have been lost over the years, although seed is still available for yellow, brown, beige, red-brown, white, and two mottled varie-

Table 4. Protein Scores of Several Tepary-Cereal Combinations

Whole Meat Combinations	Percent Protein of the Diet	Protein Score*
Tepary 67%–Wheat 33%	21.1%	95
Tepary 67%–Corn 33%	17.4	92
Tepary 50%–Wheat 50%	19.5	93
Tepary 50%–Corn 50%	16.9	97
Tepary 100%	25.0	74
Wheat 100%	14.0	56
Corn 100%	8.8	46

*A score of 100 relates to a perfect percentage amino acid pattern of a hypothetical protein assumed to be optimal for human growth and development by the Food and Agriculture Organization of the United Nations, Committee on Protein Requirements.
    From J. C. Scheerens, A. M. Tinsley, I. R. Abbas, C. W. Wever, and J. W. Berry, The Nutritional Significance of Tepary Bean Consumption, *Desert Plants* 5(1):11–14.

Table 5. Nutritive Value of Various Legumes

Variety	Protein	Fats	Carbohydrates	Calories per grams
Tepary, wild	24.5%	1.4%	*	*
Tepary, domesticated	23.2	0.8	59.0%	320
Lima beans	19.7	1.1	64.8	341
Kidney beans	22.1	1.7	61.4	341
Lentils	24.2	1.8	60.8	346
Garbanzos (chickpeas)	20.1	4.5	61.5	358

*Not available
    Compiled from Scheerens et al. (1983). Tepary values are based on research by Gary Nabhan.

ties. Beige and white teparies are grown commercially and are available in northern Mexico, in border towns, on Indian reservations, and in some Southwestern natural foods stores. The white ones taste similar to other small white beans, while the darker variety has a heartier flavor.

Properly cooked, teparies are as delicious as any other bean, and when combined in proportions of half-and-half with wheat or corn, have a protein score just slightly less than that of eggs, the standard by which all proteins are measured. They can be an important food for anyone trying to cut down on meat while maintaining a high-protein diet.

Sophisticated methods of plant breeding have made it possible for scientists to transfer specific traits from one plant to another. Besides being drought-tolerant, teparies set seed and mature quickly, taking full advantage of short wet periods. They are also tolerant of common bean blight. Some experimenters have already done work in crossing teparies with other beans to promote these desirable traits.

Persons interested in more tepary information might enjoy the Spring 1983 issue of *Desert Plants*, which is devoted entirely to the history, biology, and cultivation of this unusual bean. (*Desert Plants* is published by the University of Arizona for the Boyce Thompson Southwestern Arboretum, P.O. Box AB, Superior, AZ 85273.)

Harvesting and Cleaning

If you live in a dry climate and cannot find teparies for sale in your area, you might want to try growing your own. (See sources listed in the Appendix.)

When most of the pods are dry on the plants in the fall, you can pull up the plants, roots and all, or cut off the tops of the plants and leave the roots with their nitrogen-fixing nodules in the ground to enrich the soil. Let the plants dry in the sun for about a week. When they are completely dry, you can spread them on a canvas and beat them with a stick to separate the pods from the plants and then the beans from the pods. On a breezy day, put the beans and small chaff on a tray and toss them into the wind over a canvas. The wind will blow away most of the chaff.

John Withee, a New England bean collector and grower, suggests that anyone wanting to thresh small amounts of beans can construct a strong, funnel-like bag, tie the bottom of the bag closed and fill it with dried bean plants. Tie a rope around the big end of the bundle, throw it over a tree branch to secure it, and beat the bag with a stick until the beans fall to the bottom of the bag.

Using the rope, pull the bag up higher and hope for a breeze. Put a canvas under the bag and open the small end just a little. If luck is with you, the beans will trickle out and the chaff will blow away.

Presoaking—the Controversy

Because teparies seem to dry out more completely than other beans, it is essential that they be presoaked before cooking. Beans which have been stored a while should soak about twelve hours. Very fresh beans need less soaking and have even been known to start sprouting during a long soak. During the soaking, they will absorb quite a quantity of water. The more water they take up, the easier they will be to cook. You can figure that two cups of dried beans will swell to about five cups during soaking.

Some controversy surrounds the question of what to do with the soaking water that is not absorbed. Some people think that this contains important nutrients and should be retained and used as cooking liquid.

L. B. Rockland of the Western Regional Research Center of the U.S. Department of Agriculture, however, has been looking into bean-cooking methods and feels that the dried beans should be soaked, rinsed, and drained, then cooked and drained again. He contends that the water contains anti-nutritional substances that inhibit the utilization of proteins and that discarding the water does not appreciably change the mineral and vitamin content of the bean dish.

If you are using beans which have been stored for more than half a year, it will be helpful to add ⅛ teaspoon baking soda to the water for each cup of beans to be soaked.

Cooking Hints

I have always had difficulty estimating the exact length of time it might take a pot of teparies to cook, a fact I formerly blamed on my forgetfulness and inattention to detail. I have recently been most delighted to discover that the fault lies not with me, but with the nature of the bean itself. New studies have shown that cooking times for teparies vary much more widely than times for other beans. Once again, science has validated folk knowledge.

Although cooking times may fluctuate depending on freshness, location of the fields, type of tepary, and other yet undiscovered factors, it can generally be assumed that teparies will take considerably longer to cook than other beans.

With a heavy cast iron pot or an electric slow cooker, plan on eight to twelve hours of cooking although beans stored for many years may take even longer. A pressure cooker will complete the job in anywhere from one-half hour to an hour and fifteen minutes. Never fill a pressure cooker more than half full and use at least two quarts of water.

Some bean cooking experts suggest bringing water to a boil in a pot and then adding the beans as a method of quickly softening the seed coat. If you find you must add water during cooking, it should be hot water because reduction in cooking temperature seems to have a toughening effect on the beans. Also, salt should be added only toward the end of the cooking time as it has a toughening effect on beans.

You should also understand that a tepary that has finally become soft is not necessarily a fully cooked bean. You must continue cooking the teparies until they have lost their starchy, raw flavor, which, with conventional methods, may be as long as two additional hours.

It is at this point that the creativity starts. Too many of us palefaces who have adopted teparies from the Bean People have done more harm than good in attempts to introduce them to our own race. Blinded by our delight with their nutritional and horticultural aspects, we have relied too heavily on novelty and left the seasoning to a last-minute bit of this and dash of that and served them unadorned from a big pot.

The results have too often been bland, uninteresting, and even undercooked. It is clear that for teparies to be regarded as an acceptable food in the fast-approaching next century, they will have to be incorporated into a cuisine more contemporary and varied than that relished by the O'odham a hundred years ago.

The following recipes are some suggestions for especially delicious uses for teparies. A creative cook can come up with many more.

Remember, however, that as with other beans, teparies should be fully cooked before the addition of molasses, brown sugar, tomatoes, tomato sauce, catsup, or vinegar. When added during cooking, these ingredients tend to have a hardening effect.

Although teparies do take considerably longer to prepare than most of our modern convenience foods, the problem need not lie in the way of greater popular acceptance for teparies. Whatever cooking method you prefer, it makes sense to cook three or four times as many beans as you will need for one day, and divide the remainder into portions to be frozen for future fast-food meals.

If the following two bean combinations find their way into the lunch box, they can be called sandwich spreads. If they are used as hors d'oeuvres, they can take the dressed-up name of "pâté." For presentation as an appetizer, serve with tiny pickles sliced lengthwise and crisp crackers or crusty French bread.

White Tepary and Pork Spread
Makes Two-and-a-Half Cups

Because teparies take so long to cook, it would be ridiculous to cook only the small amount needed for this recipe. Instead, cook a big pot of beans and use portions in several different recipes.

1 medium-sized carrot	1 bay leaf
1 rib celery	½ teaspoon thyme leaves
1 onion	¼ cup dry white wine
1 shoulder pork chop	Salt and pepper
1½ cups cooked white teparies	

Coarsely chop carrot, celery, and onion. Place in a heavy, covered saucepan with the pork chop, beans, bayleaf, and thyme. Add water to cover. Bring to a boil over medium heat, then reduce heat to simmer. When pork and vegetables are done, remove pork and reserve. Add wine. Boil uncovered and stir often until liquid evaporates.

Debone meat and chop coarsely. Whirl in a food processor or blender until fine. Add beans, vegetables, and broth and process until very smooth. Add salt and pepper to taste.

Tepary Vegetarian Pâté

This is so rich it tastes sinful; so healthy you can dine on hors d'oeuvres alone. The best appliance to use is a food mill or food processor. A blender can be used but you will need to add more bean broth to make the mixture wetter.

1 stalk celery, chopped
1 large carrot, chopped
1 onion, chopped
1 or 2 cloves garlic, minced
1 tablespoon olive oil
¼ cup sunflower seeds
2 cups cooked teparies or
    other beans

2 tablespoons wheat germ
1 tablespoon soy sauce
1 tablespoon wine vinegar
¼ teaspoon basil
¼ teaspoon oregano

Sauté celery, carrot, onion, and garlic in olive oil in medium frying pan until tender. Grind sunflower seeds to a meal in blender or mill. Combine teparies, cooked vegetables, sunflower meal, wheat germ, soy sauce, wine vinegar, and herbs and process until smooth.

Variations: Add one of the following flavor combinations or invent your own: ¼ teaspoon cumin and 2 tablespoons green taco sauce or chopped green chiles; or 2 tablespoons sherry, ¼ teaspoon nutmeg, and ¼ cup chopped pecans.

Best Bean Loaf

Serves Six to Eight

The outer covering of greens called for in this recipe not only adds texture and visual appeal, but also helps in getting the loaf out of the pan in one piece.

5 or 6 large leaves savoy cabbage or chard
1½ cups mashed tepary beans
1½ cups cooked bulgur wheat or rice
1 cup grated zucchini
½ cup chopped onion
1 tablespoon soy sauce
¼ cup whole wheat bread crumbs
2 beaten eggs
1 tablespoon dry basil
¼ teaspoon salt
¼ teaspoon pepper
Parsley and black olives for garnish (optional)

Grease a 9 × 5-inch loaf pan. Preheat oven to 350 degrees F. In a large saucepan of boiling salted water, blanch the cabbage or chard leaves for about three minutes or until they are pliable. Drain the leaves in a colander and pat them dry. Line prepared pan with as many of the leaves as are needed, smooth side down, to cover the bottom and sides, leaving enough overhang to fold over and cover the top.

Try to mash the teparies with as little liquid as possible. In a large bowl, combine teparies with the remaining ingredients and mix well. Spoon the mixture into the loaf pan, rap the pan sharply on the counter to expel any bubbles, and smooth the top. Fold the overhanging leaves over the mixture and cover the pan with foil.

Place the loaf pan in a larger flat pan, pour one to two inches of hot water into the larger pan and bake the loaf in preheated oven for one hour or until a toothpick inserted in the center comes out clean. Let the loaf stand for about ten minutes to settle. Unmold on a platter, blot up any liquid with paper towels. Garnish the platter with parsley and black olives, and slice the loaf with a very sharp knife.

Serve with a sauce such as spiced tomato or yogurt flavored with mustard, garlic and tahini.

Dad's Basic Beans

My father was in the food business all his life, managing restaurants and selling groceries. He was an excellent cook, too, specializing in Midwestern-style American food. He used Great Northern or pea beans in this recipe. I have tried it with teparies, and it is equally delicious.

½ pound beans
1 cup tops and leaves of
   celery, chopped
1 cup chopped onion
1 carrot, finely grated
1 large clove garlic, minced

½ small can chopped green
   chiles
½ teaspoon black pepper
Salt to taste
3 slices bacon
3 or 4 very thin slices onion

Soak beans overnight. Drain and rinse. Combine with two quarts water and all other ingredients except bacon and sliced onion. Cook in a pressure cooker at fifteen pounds for forty-five minutes or until done (or cook in a crockpot or heavy pot on the stove until tender). When cooked, salt to taste. Transfer to a baking dish and cover with the bacon and sliced onion. Bake at 350 degrees F. for forty-five minutes.

Layered Tepary Enchiladas

Serves Two

The combination of teparies, corn, and cheese makes this dish rich in protein without meat.

Oil for frying
6 corn tortillas
2 cups cooked teparies
1 cup cooked corn kernels
1 small can tomato sauce

Chile powder or chile paste, to taste
¼ teaspoon cumin, or to taste
½ cup shredded longhorn or jack cheese

Heat ¼ inch oil in small frying pan and fry tortillas one by one briefly until limp but not crisp. In a medium saucepan, combine teparies, corn kernels, and tomato sauce; heat. Season to taste with chile and cumin. For each individual serving, place a tortilla on a plate, add a layer of beans, then repeat twice, ending with beans. Top with shredded cheese.

The following two recipes use the humble desert tepary in recipes from rich and flavorful Italian cuisine.

Tuscany-Style Beans

Serves Two to Four

2 tablespoons butter
3 tablespoons olive oil
2 cups cooked drained teparies, preferably white

1½ teaspoons dried sage
1 large or 2 small tomatoes
Salt and pepper

Heat together the butter and olive oil in a large frying pan or saucepan. Add the beans and sage. Chop tomato coarsely and whirl in a blender until pureed. Add to beans. Season to taste with salt and pepper. Serve hot.

Bean Bread

Makes One Loaf

The presence of mashed beans in this recipe tends to inhibit the formation of gluten in the flour. Gluten is the substance that holds the bread crumbs together and makes nice slices. Development of gluten can be encouraged by thorough beating of the dough, however, so use a food processor, a table mixer, or your good strong arms. The dough is a bit too thick for a hand-held mixer.

½ cup shortening or margarine
½ cup sugar
1 egg
1½ cups moist mashed beans
½ teaspoon salt

1¾ cups sifted flour
2 teaspoons baking powder
½ teaspoon cinnamon
½ teaspoon nutmeg
¼ teaspoon ground ginger
¼ cup chopped nuts, if desired

Grease and flour a 9×5-inch loaf pan. Preheat oven to 350 degrees F. Cream shortening; add sugar, beating until fluffy. Add egg and beat. Add beans which have been mashed with enough bean broth to make them moist but not soupy; beat. Add flour, baking powder, and spices and beat for four minutes. Stir in nuts if desired.

Spread in prepared loaf pan and bake in preheated oven for forty-five minutes or until a toothpick inserted in the center comes out clean.

Pasta e Fagioli

Serves Eight

8 ounces shell macaroni
3 tablespoons olive oil
2 cups sliced carrot
1 clove garlic, crushed
2 cups diced, peeled
   tomatoes
1 teaspoon dried basil leaves
½ teaspoon dried oregano
   leaves

¼ teaspoon pepper
Salt to taste
2½ cups cooked teparies
1½ cups bean liquid
1 cup steamed broccoli
   spears
Grated Parmesan cheese

Cook macaroni following package directions. Meanwhile, in hot oil in a large skillet, sauté onion, carrot, and garlic until soft but not brown. Add tomato, herbs, salt, and pepper to taste. Cover pan and cook gently for fifteen minutes.

In large saucepan or kettle, combine beans, macaroni, and vegetable mixture. Add the bean liquid. Bring to a boil, cover, and simmer fifteen minutes until flavors blend. Stir often to prevent sticking. At the end, add broccoli spears, heat, and turn into attractive serving dish. Sprinkle with Parmesan cheese.

Camping Beans

Serves Four

"Instant" or precooked beans are a very ancient form of traveling food. Sheila Moller contributed this recipe to the Sonoran Heritage Recipe Exchange, part of a class on desert foods.

2 cups teparies or other beans
2 garlic cloves, minced

1 onion, chopped
Salt and pepper to taste

Clean the beans and soak them overnight. Drain, rinse, place in a saucepan with a heavy lid and cover with water. Add the garlic and onion. Cook over low heat until beans are soft. Smash some of the beans against the side of the kettle or crockpot with the back of a spoon, then stir them into the cooking liquid to form a very thick, rich broth. Stir often and be careful that the beans do not burn. Season to taste.

Spread the beans on a cookie sheet or jelly roll pan and allow to dry out thoroughly. After the beans are dry, they can be broken into chunks, placed in plastic bags, and taken on a backpacking or camping trip. To fix them in camp, add water, heat and eat. Makes 2 cups dried beans.

CHILES

Compared to some of the other foods in this book, the most common type of domesticated chile is a relative newcomer to the southwestern United States. Although a growing body of evidence indicates that prehistoric people of this area enjoyed a lively trade with people in Central Mexico, exchanging turquoise and parrot feathers and copper bells, apparently none of the southern traders brought along any of the spicy peppers that to this very day distinguish the cuisine of the land of the Aztecs.

The Indians of the "northern" wilderness had to rely on the tiny pea-sized wild chiltepins until the Spanish explorers of the sixteenth century brought with them the larger chiles of the south.

Although Mexican markets display a colorful and often bewildering variety of chiles, our choices on this side of the border are relatively few.

The most widely available chile is the Anaheim (also called the California and New Mexico chile) which is 5 to 8 inches long and about 1 to 1½ inches in diameter. In its green stage it is known as "chile verde" and is available fresh or canned. If left on the bush, this same chile will turn bright red, after which it is usually dried and strung on long loops or "ristras," or it is ground into a fine powder and sold as a spice. The Anaheim is a medium hot chile; the flavor, however, varies depending on growing conditions. (New Mexican chile farmers pride themselves on the extra pungency of their chile peppers.)

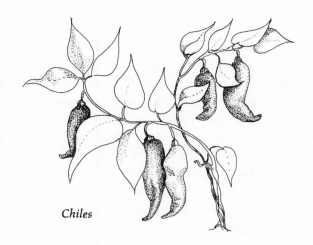

Chiles

The next most popular type of chile is the jalapeño, which is usually marketed when it is dark green. The fresh peppers are about ¾ inch in diameter and 2½ inches long and are guaranteed to light a fire in your mouth. They are also available canned and are usually labeled "hot." It is important not to mistake this type of chile for the much milder Anaheim or "green chile"; *they are not interchangeable in recipes.*

Other chiles occasionally found in grocery stores in the Southwest are yellow peppers, which are very hot and sometimes pickled or used in sauces; ancho and mulatto chiles, usually dried and used for molé sauces; and serrano chiles, tiny green chiles even smaller and hotter than jalapeños.

Some people believe you can gauge the hotness of a chile by the shape of its tip: the more pointed the end, the hotter the chile. It is possible to regulate the spiciness of a dish by using more or less chile to taste. Discarding the seeds and removing the pithy ribs inside the chile will give a milder taste.

NOTE: Unless otherwise indicated, the term "green chiles" in these recipes refers to the milder Anaheim-style chiles.

Peeling Green Chiles

Preheat the broiling unit in your oven. Wash the chiles and make a small slit in the stem end with the point of a knife. Lay chiles out on a broiling pan and place in position closest to heat. Turn chiles frequently until brown and blistered on all sides. Remove from oven and let chiles cool for about 30 seconds, then place in a paper or plastic bag to steam for about 10 minutes. (If using plastic, try one chile first; if it melts the plastic, wait a bit longer for the rest of the chiles.)

While wearing plastic gloves (the thin kind are best), peel the chiles from the stem end. Remove the seeds. The chiles are now ready to be used, or they may be stored in the refrigerator.

To Freeze: Do not peel the chiles; rather, freeze whole broiled chiles. Defrost at room temperature. The skins will slip off.

Pear and Pepper Relish
Makes Three Pints

This is a sweet-hot treat that can turn an ordinary meal into something special. Save a few jars back to give as gifts for those times when you need something in a hurry. Wear rubber gloves when cutting the jalapeños.

8 firm-ripe pears	1½ cups cider vinegar
2 jalapeño peppers	1½ cups honey
2 large green bell peppers	1 teaspoon finely minced
2 large red bell peppers	fresh ginger
1 large onion	½ teaspoon salt

Core and chop the unpeeled pears. Seed and chop the jalapeños and green and red bell peppers. Chop the onion. The chopping can be done in a food processor, but do not overprocess.

In a kettle that holds at least five quarts, combine the chopped pears, bell pepper, onion, vinegar, honey, ginger, and salt. Bring to a boil and simmer, uncovered, until reduced to 6 cups—about one hour. As mixture thickens, stir often to prevent sticking.

Pour into sterilized jars and seal with canning lids. Even unsealed, this relish can be stored in the refrigerator for several months.

Jalapeño Jelly

Makes About Five-and-a-Half Cups

Use rubber gloves when working with jalapeños; otherwise the fieriness of these little peppers can easily be transferred from fingers to eyes or lips even after you have washed your hands. The finished jelly is spicy but not overwhelmingly hot. Try it with cream cheese on crackers for a quick but delicious hors d'oeuvre.

5 cups sugar	½ cup chopped jalapeños
1½ cups cider vinegar	6 ounces liquid pectin
½ cup chopped green bell pepper	(Certo)

Sterilize jelly jars and lids by boiling in water for fifteen minutes. Measure sugar into large five-quart saucepan. In blender combine ½ cup vinegar, bell pepper, and jalapeños. Blend until pepper pieces are very fine. Add to sugar. Rinse out blender with remaining vinegar, and add to saucepan. Bring mixture to a rolling boil and boil two minutes. All at once pour in pectin, return to a full boil and boil one minute, stirring constantly. Remove from heat, stir and skim off foam. Pour into sterilized jars and seal with wax or canning lids.

Green Chile Salsa

Makes One Pint

The basis for this recipe is tomatillos, also called husk to-matoes, which are available in Mexican grocery stores and can be found increasingly often in local supermarkets. This unusual vegetable, which is growing in popularity, looks like a small green tomato and is covered with a thin papery husk. The pulp is more dense and less juicy than a regular tomato. Canned tomatillos can be substituted for the fresh variety but you will have to adapt the liquid requirements of the recipe somewhat to accommodate whatever juices are included in the canned product. If you want to try growing your own tomatillos, you will find seed sources in the Appendix.

¼ cup chopped green onion
4 cloves garlic, minced
  or crushed
2 tablespoons oil
9 or 10 large tomatillos
  (2 cups ground)
½ cup water

¼ cup chopped fresh or
  canned green chiles
¼ to ½ teaspoon minced
  jalapeño pepper, if desired
¼ cup chopped fresh
  cilantro (coriander)

In a one-quart saucepan with a heavy bottom and lid, sauté the green onion and garlic in the oil until just transparent. Remove husks from tomatillos, wash, and chop in quarters. Grind until fine in a food processor fitted with a steel blade or in a blender. (If you use a blender, it is best to process the tomatillos in two batches, using the half cup of water.) Add ground tomatillos to the onion mixture along with the water (if you have not already added it to the tomatillos), the chopped green chiles, and the jalapeño. Stir, cover, and simmer on low heat for about twenty minutes. Add cilantro and cook another five minutes.

Chile Cheese Enchiladas

Serves Six

This high-protein meatless dish uses both red and green chiles. If you are trying to cut down on dairy fat, substitute yogurt or mashed tofu for all or part of the sour cream and cheese.

1½ cups sour cream
1½ cups small curd cottage
    cheese
1 tablespoon instant onion
    soup mix
¾ cup sliced green onion
1 can (7 ounces) green chiles
    or 4 fresh roasted and
    peeled green chiles

2½ cups shredded jack
    cheese
1½ cups red chile sauce or
1 can (10 ounces) enchilada
    sauce

Preheat oven to 350 degrees F. In a bowl combine the sour cream, cottage cheese, instant onion soup mix, and all but ¼ cup of the green onions. Heat ¼ inch oil in a frying pan until hot. Briefly fry each tortilla until limp (a few seconds). Drain tortillas. Seed the chiles and remove and discard the ribs for a mild flavor. Separate into twelve strips.

Reserve ½ cup of the shredded cheese for garnish. Roughly divide remaining cheese and sour cream mixture into twelve portions. Fill center of each tortilla with one portion of sour cream, one portion of grated jack cheese, and a chile strip. Roll tortillas and place seam-side down in a 9 × 13-inch pan. Pour red chile sauce over the enchiladas, sprinkle with the reserved cheese, and garnish with a thin line of reserved green onions. Bake in preheated oven for thirty minutes.

Chile Cheese Puff

Serves Three to Four

My mother raved about this recipe for years before she could get me to try it. I was going through my "authentic" phase, and the name did not sound like anything a Mexican grandma would cook. Do not be as irrational as I was; whip this up the next time you need a light dish for brunch or supper.

2 cans (4 ounces each) whole green chiles or 6 to 7 fresh peeled chiles
¼ pound jack cheese
2 cups milk
4 eggs

⅓ cup instant flour (Wondra)
½ teaspoon salt
Dash pepper
½ pound grated longhorn cheese

Grease a 7 × 11-inch baking dish. Preheat oven to 350 degrees F. Clean seeds and ribs from chiles, trying not to tear chiles. Cut jack cheese in strips and stuff chiles. Arrange flat in a row in prepared baking dish. In a medium bowl, beat eggs; add flour, milk, salt, pepper, and combine. Pour over chiles. Sprinkle with grated longhorn cheese. Bake in preheated oven for forty-five to fifty minutes until puffed and golden.

Zuni Crockpot Stew

Serves Four to Six

This recipe is so simple I almost hate to give away the secret. Serve with flour tortillas or crusty bread and a green salad.

1 large onion, sliced
2 to 2½ pound pork butt, trimmed of all fat
½ cup water
1 can (15 ounces) garbanzo beans

1 can (4 ounces) green chiles or ½ cup fresh chiles
Salt and pepper to taste

In the morning, place onion, pork butt, and water in crockpot on low and go about your day. When you are ready for dinner, break up the meat and remove any bones and fat. Add drained garbanzos. Seed and devein the chiles and chop or separate into strips. Turn crockpot to high and simmer stew until heated through. If you wish, you can thicken the liquid with a little flour mixed with water. Season to taste with salt and pepper.

All Wrong Chile

Serves Four

The reason this chile is "all wrong"—well, mostly wrong, anyway—is that true chile aficionados never use beans in their chile. If some maverick does use beans the choice is usually brown pintos or red kidneys. Most chile recipes call for red peppers, although green ones may sometimes be included as well. The meat is generally beef, although pork, venison, or even javelina (wild pig) is sometimes used. All Wrong Chile uses beans—white teparies; green chiles only; and turkey. But the joke is on all the purists. This chile tastes great!

5 cups cooked white teparies   1 cup strong turkey broth
   or white pea beans and   1 to 2 cups cut-up turkey
   cooking broth   1 can (4 ounces) chopped
½ cup chopped onion   green chiles
1 or 2 cloves garlic, minced   ½ teaspoon cumin
2 tablespoons oil   Salt and pepper to taste

Put beans and their broth into a medium-sized covered saucepan and smash some of the beans against the side of the pot with the back of a spoon. Stir mashed beans into the broth to thicken it. In a skillet brown the chopped onion and minced garlic in a little oil. Add to the beans along with the turkey broth, turkey, green chiles, cumin, and salt and pepper to taste. Simmer fifteen minutes to thicken and blend flavors.

Chile Rice

Serves Four to Six

This recipe came from Byrd Baylor, well-known author of children's books.

½ pound jack cheese
1 large can green chiles
   or ½ cup roasted and
   peeled fresh chiles

1 pint sour cream
3 cups cooked rice
Black olives and pimientos
   for garnish

Preheat oven to 350 degrees F. Butter a 1½-quart casserole. Cut jack cheese into long slivers. Mix green chiles and sour cream together. In a casserole, layer rice, chile and sour cream mixture, and cheese, ending with sour cream. Decorate top with sliced olives and pimientos. Bake in preheated oven for twenty to twenty-five minutes or until cheese has melted and casserole is warmed through.

Red Chile Puree

Makes About Two-and-a-Half Pints

12 dried red Anaheim chiles
4 cups boiling water

1 clove garlic, peeled
Sprinkle of salt

Remove the stems from the chiles and shake out and discard seeds. Rinse chiles and tear each into about three pieces. Cover with the boiling water and let set about an hour.

Put about half the chiles and half the soaking water along with the peeled garlic clove into a blender container and whirl until smooth. Empty blender into a fine strainer set over a bowl. Repeat process with remaining chiles and soaking liquid. Strain. Add salt and stir contents of bowl to blend. Freeze in recipe-size batches.

Red Chile Sauce

Makes One Pint

1 tablespoon shortening
2 tablespoons flour
1½ cups red chile puree or
  6 tablespoons chile powder

½ teaspoon garlic powder
Pinch of powdered oregano
1½ cups water
  (approximately)

In a heavy frying pan melt the shortening, add flour, and cook a few minutes until bubbly. Add chile powder or chile puree, garlic powder, and oregano. Add water to thin. Simmer fifteen to twenty minutes, stirring occasionally to prevent burning.

Variation: Add up to ½ cup of tomato sauce for a milder flavor.

CORN

In the New World—the Americas—corn has been a staple for five thousand years. People of Europe, Africa, and Asia have been eating various forms of *Zea mays* for only about five hundred years—since Christopher Columbus and other early explorers discovered the inhabitants of America and their tasty staple food and took samples back home.

Corn grows only where there are farmers to care for it. It grows anew from seed each year. Some annuals reseed themselves, but corn must be planted by a human being at exactly the right time. And, unlike most of our food plants, nothing similar to corn grows in the wild. Even its closest relative—teosinte—does not produce cobs and kernels.

That leaves us with a mystery. If there was no wild form of corn for the ancient populations to develop and domesticate, how did it come into being as a food plant? The origins of corn have become a major cause of speculation in the botanical community. Many scientists have devoted their entire professional lives to the problem.

Finding the answers is of more than just academic interest. Horticulturalists involved in the process of cross-breeding plants to produce new and more productive strains, often rely on wild relatives of our domesticated plants when searching for desirable characteristics.

All of the corn varieties we have today are descendants of the

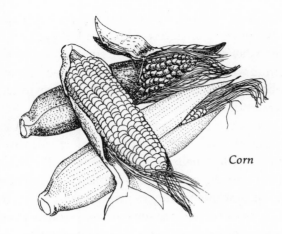

Corn

sweet corn, dent corn, flint corn, flour corn, and popcorn that Columbus found, and most of the commercial hybrids grown in the United States today are based on a very few types. The Green Revolution, as it is sometimes known, has produced corn that does extremely well under optimal growing conditions but is also very vulnerable to disease.

Because all strains of corn are so closely inbred, one virus can have a devastating effect on an entire crop. In the summer of 1970, southern U.S. farmers faced a near disaster as the Southern Leaf Blight Fungus raced through their crops at the rate of fifty miles or more a day. Plant breeders knew that to prevent the recurrence of such tragedies, work had to be done to make the strains hardier.

Then, in the late 1970s, an amazing series of coincidences occurred that began to change the face of corn hybridizing.

In class one day at the University of Guadalajara, a Mexican botany professor told her students that a North American colleague was looking for a perennial form of one of corn's near relatives. One of her students, Rafael Guzman, found the plant and began to grow it. When another student told Guzman of a stand of the plant near his family's village, Guzman went to check it out. While he was collecting the seeds, an old man rode by on a mule and fell to talking with the visitor. He told the young botanist that he knew a place in the mountains where a greater number of the plant grew. Guzman followed his directions and after a day's journey found the stand. What he did not know at the time was that the old man had directed him to an as yet undescribed species of plant—a corn relative previously unknown to scientists.

Subsequent experiments have shown that this plant can be successfully crossed with our modern corn. Horticulturalists involved with the project believe that the genes of the wild plant can improve our inbred strains of corn in many ways. There will be advantages in time and money to growing perennial crops of corn which can be harvested for several years without replanting. The new plant also carries resistance to several viral diseases and to such insect pests as corn earworms, stalk borers, and rootworms, and it may contribute to stronger stalks and roots and greater tolerance to poorly drained soil.

Of course, not all the types of corn grown today are touchy hybrids. Some farmers, mainly those who work on a smaller scale, have continued to grow non-hybrid varieties of corn— types which have over generations adapted to very special climatic conditions.

In fact, there are more than two hundred varieties of New World corn. Some of the more interesting of these are the Indian varieties which come in brilliant colors including red and even blue. There is even a flour corn developed by the Pimas and Tohono O'odhams which matures in from fifty to seventy-five days when planted in the July–August rainy season.

A small but growing group of individuals is working hard to make sure these seed stocks are preserved for the hardiness and diversity they contribute to our agricultural tradition. (See the Appendix for lists of seed companies and sources for blue corn meal.)

All this attention paid to corn means more to average Americans than they might realize. U.S. farmers produce three times as much corn as they do wheat—5.5 billion bushels each year. We eat our share of it in corn on the cob, corn bread, and popcorn but because much of our country's corn crop goes for animal feed, each of us eats about a pound of corn at each meal in the form of meat, eggs, and dairy products.

In her book *Diet for a Small Planet*, Frances Moore Lappé estimates that, excluding exports, about one-half of our harvested acreage goes to feed livestock. These cattle, pigs, and chickens consume ten times the grain Americans do directly, and yet, on the average, for each fifteen pounds of grain these animals eat, they give us back only one pound of food for our plates.

Corn is a nutritious grain although low in lysine and tryptophane (which converts to niacin), both of which are found in abundance in beans and dairy products. Dishes which combine these food groups can form the basis of nutritious meals. Many Americans are now beginning to see the wisdom of eating more corn directly in such recipes as the ones here and eating a little less of grain which has been processed into meat and picked up a burden of cholesterol on the way.

What we call sweet corn has been bred to have a thin skin on the kernels and is ready to eat after a short cooking time. Kernels of flour corn and other varieties we lump under "field corn" have a tough seed coat when mature. These varieties can sometimes be used for roasting ears if picked very young or "green." They can also be made into hominy by a process which loosens the tough seed coats so that they slip off.

Corn Salad

Serves Four

With the addition of cheese, meat, or fish, this can become a main dish salad for hot weather meals.

8 ears corn, husked
½ cup olive oil
¼ cup cider vinegar
1 tablespoon fresh lemon juice
2 teaspoons Dijon-style
   mustard
¼ cup minced parsley
2 tablespoons minced fresh
   basil leaves or
2 teaspoons dried basil

Salt and pepper, to taste
3 tablespoons sliced
   black olives
3 tomatoes cut in wedges
4 green onions, sliced
1 green pepper, chopped fine
Lettuce

Fill a large kettle with water and bring to a boil. Add the corn and cover the kettle. Return to boil. Remove from heat and let stand about eight minutes. Drain and cool. Cut kernels off cobs. In a large bowl, combine olive oil, vinegar, lemon juice, mustard, parsley, basil and salt and pepper to taste. Mix until well blended. Add corn, green pepper, black olives, green onions, and tomato wedges. Toss with dressing. Line a salad bowl with lettuce and pile corn salad in the center.

Fresh Corn Pudding

Serves Four to Six

16 to 18 ears very fresh corn
1 egg, separated
3 tablespoons butter or
   margarine

2 teaspoons sugar
1 teaspoon salt
Sprinkle of garlic powder, if
   desired

Preheat oven to 350 degrees F. Grease a shallow one-quart baking dish. With a sharp knife, slit down the center of each row of corn kernels. With the dull edge of the knife, press out the pulp and juice into a bowl to make about 3 cups. Add egg yolk, sugar, salt, and garlic powder, if desired. Melt 2 tablespoons of the butter and add.

In a small bowl, beat egg white until stiff peaks form. Fold into the corn mixture. Turn into greased baking dish and dot with remaining butter. Bake in preheated oven for forty-five minutes or until golden brown.

Corn and Leek Soup
Serves Three

This is an excellent use for leftover corn on the cob.

2 ears corn, cooked	1 cup chicken stock, canned
1 leek	or fresh
1 garlic clove, minced	2 teaspoons minced fresh dill
2 tablespoons butter	or 1 teaspoon dried
2 tablespoons bacon fat	¼ cup yogurt
¼ cup dry sherry	1 cup milk

Remove kernels from the cobs using a sharp knife. Melt the butter and bacon fat in a saucepan. Slice the leek finely and sauté in the fat along with the corn kernels and garlic until leek is transparent. Add sherry, dill, and stock. Cover the pan and cook five minutes. Transfer the vegetables to a blender container, and puree. Return to saucepan, add milk and yogurt, and combine. Heat, being careful not to boil. Salt and pepper to taste. To serve, ladle into bowls and sprinkle with more fresh dill.

Corn Stew with Blue Corn Dumplings

Serves Six

This stew is similar to those cooked every day by Hopi women who still live in the ancient villages perched atop high, narrow mesas in northeastern Arizona.

2 pounds stewing beef, cut
    into 1-inch cubes
2 tablespoons lard or oil
1 medium-sized onion,
    chopped
1 small green bell pepper,
    chopped

1 tablespoon red chile powder
4 cups corn kernels
1 medium-sized pumpkin,
    peeled and cubed
2 tablespoons whole wheat
    flour, if desired
Salt to taste

In a large heavy pot with a tight-fitting lid, sauté meat in fat, one-third at a time, until lightly browned. Transfer meat to plate. Sauté onion and green pepper in same pan until onion is transparent. Return meat to pan; add chile powder and enough water to cover meat and simmer for one hour and thirty minutes, or until nearly tender.

Add corn, pumpkin, and salt to taste. Simmer until tender. Drop Blue Corn Dumpling batter (recipe to follow) by spoonfuls onto stew. Cover and simmer for fifteen minutes. Remove dumplings to a plate and keep warm. If gravy is too thin, thicken with 2 tablespoons whole wheat flour mixed with 2 tablespoons water.

Blue Corn Dumplings

2 cups ground blue cornmeal
2 teaspoons baking powder
1 teaspoon salt

¼ cup shortening
¾ cup milk

In a medium bowl, combine cornmeal, baking powder, and salt; cut in shortening until mixture looks like meal. Add milk to form a soft but stiff dough, ready to be cooked in stew broth.

Corn Crepes

Makes Two Dozen

During the year I spent in Africa I would often get the typical Southwesterner's craving for Mexican food. Unfortunately, the closest tortilla was half a globe away, so we settled on something like this made from a recipe given to me by a missionary. Actually, these crepes are good in their own right, not just as a substitute for tortillas. Try blue corn for an authentic New Mexico-style touch.

3 eggs
½ cup all-purpose flour
1 cup yellow or blue cornmeal
2¼ cups milk

1½ tablespoons salad oil
½ teaspoon chile powder
¼ teaspoon salt
Butter, margarine, or oil

Combine all ingredients in a blender and whirl until smooth. Heat a crepe pan over medium heat; add ¼ teaspoon butter or margarine or a brushing of corn oil. Pour in about 2 tablespoons of batter, tilting pan so batter flows evenly over bottom. Cook until edges are lightly browned, then turn to cook other side. Stack crepes as finished on a clean tea towel or plate. Stir batter frequently since the cornmeal tends to settle.

To Fill Crepes: Mix your favorite recipe for meat or cheese filling. Use ¼ cup for each crepe and roll. Place seam side down in a greased flat pottery dish or baking pan. Heat in a 350 degree F. oven for about ten minutes. Sprinkle with more grated cheese and heat until melted.

Survival Corn Cakes

Makes about Ten Cakes

When I was teaching a class in southwestern foods, I asked the students to bring in their own favorite regional recipes. Denise Lasley contributed this one, suggesting these corn cakes were a good backpacking staple.

¾ cup corn meal
2 tablespoons raw sunflower seeds or piñon nuts
2 tablespoons Parmesan cheese
1 tablespoon soy flour (or mesquite meal)
1 tablespoon ground sesame seeds
1 tablespoon wheat bran
Salt to taste
1 tablespoon corn oil
½ cup water

Mix dry ingredients together in a medium bowl. In a small pan, boil 1 tablespoon of corn oil in ½ cup water. Add liquid to dry mixture and combine. Heat oven to 350 degrees F. and lightly oil two baking sheets while dough cools. Form dough into thin patties not over ¼ inch thick. Place them on oiled baking sheets. Bake the rounds until bottoms are crisp and well-browned. Turn the cakes over and bake until other side browns. Serve with honey.

Fresh Corn Hominy

Makes Two Quarts

This recipe is the way Indian and pioneer women turned their hard corn into succulent hominy.

1 quart wood ashes or corncob ashes or
4 heaping tablespoons powdered lime
4 quarts water
2 quarts fresh corn kernels

In a large granite or enamel pan (not metal), add the ashes to the water and boil for thirty minutes. Stir until the mixture stops bubbling; strain. If using powdered lime, simply dissolve the lime in the water. Add the 2 quarts of corn kernels or as much corn as the water will cover. Cook until the hulls loosen from the kernels. Remove the corn from the heat, drain the liquid, and wash until all the lime taste is gone.

Dried Corn Hominy
Makes One Quart

This is a more modern recipe for making hominy, using dried corn.

1 quart dried corn
1½ gallons water

2 tablespoons baking soda
1 teaspoon salt

In a large enamel or stainless steel pan, place corn and 2 quarts of the water to which the baking soda has been added. Cover the pan and wait twelve hours. Simmer the contents of the pan over low heat for three hours or until hulls loosen. If necessary, add water. Drain. Rub corn until hulls are loosened. Rinse. Return corn to pan, add another 2 quarts of water, and bring to a boil. Drain and repeat the boiling and rinsing with another 2 quarts of water. Drain and stir in 1 teaspoon of salt.

Corn in a Kettle

Serves Four

Well-known fiction writer Jeanne Williams often manages to fit a camping trip into her busy schedule. A vegetarian, she likes to serve this dish for the evening meal and cooks it in a big pot or dutch oven over mesquite coals. Nobody ever misses the steaks.

1 can (16 ounces) hominy, yellow or white
1 can (16 ounces) kernel corn or 2 cups fresh cut corn
1 can (4 ounces) green chiles or ½ cup fresh chiles
2 cups grated cheese

Drain hominy and corn. Chop green chiles. Beginning with hominy, make alternate layers of hominy, corn, chiles, and cheese, ending with cheese. Bake, covered, until cheese is melted and vegetables are warmed through. In a home oven bake thirty minutes at 350 degrees F. May be easily doubled or tripled.

Posole
(Pork and Hominy Stew)

Serves Six to Eight

People who have lived or traveled in New Mexico find that long after they have left the state, the memory of posole lingers: they often get a distinct yearning for this simple yet very special dish. The most authentic versions use Mexican hominy (white corn soaked in lime water, also called nixtamal), which is available fresh from Mexican grocery stores or tortilla factories. Dried Mexican hominy can also be purchased by mail order from several shops (see Appendix). Canned hominy also works.

Plan to prepare this dish the day before you wish to serve it so that you can remove some of the extra fat when the soup is chilled. The extra time also allows the flavors to blend.

2 cups dried posole or
   3 cups fresh posole or
   2 pounds canned hominy,
   drained
2 large fresh pork hocks,
   split into two or three
   pieces each

2 large garlic cloves, minced
1 teaspoon oregano
1 dried red chile pod
Salt to taste
Red Chile Sauce (see page
   159)

Place dried posole in a large pot and add 5 cups of water. Bring to a boil and cook for two minutes. Turn off heat, cover pot, and let stand for one to two hours.

Place pork hocks and two quarts of water in large pot. Add soaked dried posole or fresh posole, garlic, oregano, and crumbled chile pod. (If using canned hominy, do not add it until mixture is reheated.) Simmer slowly for two to three hours until posole is soft and meat is falling off the bones. Add water as necessary. Season with salt to taste near end of cooking time.

Remove pot from heat and transfer pork hocks to a plate. When they are cool enough to handle, cut meat into small pieces, discarding skin, fat and bones. Return meat to soup and refrigerate soup overnight or at least until fat has risen to the top and congealed. Remove fat.

If using canned hominy, drain and add it to soup mixture and reheat slowly. Serve with a bowl of Red Chile Sauce.

Variation: May also be served with thinly sliced green onions and lime wedges.

PUMPKINS AND SQUASH

Like corn and beans, pumpkins and squash were not known in the Old World until Columbus and other explorers after him "discovered" them and carried them back across the ocean to Europe.

Anthropologists tell us that American Indians were eating squashes as early as 300 B.C. By one of those mysterious processes forever lost in time, some early group, or perhaps an individual, had discovered a mutant of the usually bitter wild gourds which miraculously offered flesh sweet enough to eat. Through time the early agriculturalists developed the vegetable, and knowledge of it spread.

By the time the first Spanish explorers traveled northward from the Valley of Mexico and entered what is now northern

Hopi Cushaw Squash

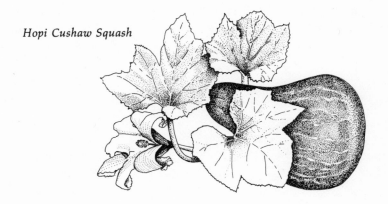

Pumpkin

Mexico and the American Southwest, the Indians they encountered all grew bountiful crops of various squashes which the Spaniards called *calabasas*.

Later, when English settlers arrived on the Atlantic Coast, they too found the native populations growing this unfamiliar vegetable. The Indians of Massachusetts called the soft-shelled varieties *askutasquash*, meaning "green things eaten green." Some of the English called the vegetables "vine apples," but eventually they adopted the Indian terminology, shortening it to "squash."

Deciding what to call the yellow-meated, hard-shelled squashes was more troublesome to the new settlers. *Sturtevant's Notes on Edible Plants* quotes a number of early writers in their literary debates on whether the large fruits should be termed "pompions, gourds, or melons."

During the intervening centuries, the confusion has persisted over just what is a squash and what a pumpkin. In common terminology we usually call the quick-growing soft-skinned varieties "summer squash" and the long-season hard-skinned types "winter squash," while reserving the term "pumpkin" for that easily distinguished orange globe associated with Halloween. Gourds are usually considered to be inedible.

Botanists, however, take a slightly different view. They lump the common pumpkin and the summer squashes together under *Cucurbita pepo* (from the Greek *pepon*, meaning "mellow, ripe"). Some of the common winter squashes, such as Hubbard, banana, butternut, and acorn, are *C. maxima.* Another variety of hard-shelled squash particularly suited for areas where the summer is hot and dry is *Cucurbita mixta*, also called Mexican pumpkin, cushaw squash, or just calabasas by the Mexican and Indian people who still grow it. It is an interesting vegetable for the home gardener because the fruits are wonderfully varied, ranging from green to dark gray to white, striped or solid, roundish or crook-necked, smooth or lumpy. Mexicans particularly relish its large seeds. (Gardeners can order seeds from suppliers listed in the Appendix.)

The recipes in this chapter use pumpkin and yellow-meated winter squash interchangeably. The so-called winter squash are usually somewhat higher in nutritive value than the summer squash and pumpkins; however, all squash provide large amounts of vitamin A.

Squash and Pumpkin Blossoms

Like the fruit they produce, squash blossoms are good in a number of dishes. If you pick only male blossoms (see illustration), you will not reduce your harvest at all, for only female flowers produce squash. The immature fruit shows at the female's base from the time the flower first opens. Some gardeners attempt to grow very large pumpkins or squash to take to the country fair, and they have to pick off all but a few blossoms to force all of the plant's strength into just a few specimens. The blossoms are full of flavor and nutrition.

The best time to pick squash blossoms is in the early morning, before they have opened. Pick them with a small section of stem attached and store them in a plastic bag in the refrigerator until you wish to cook them in the evening. (They do not store well for more than a day, two at the most.) Squash blossoms can be deep fried as fritters, stuffed, or blended into soups.

Blossom Fritters

Makes One Dozen

1 dozen blossoms
⅓ cup milk
1 beaten egg
1 tablespoon flour

1 tablespoon cornmeal
¼ teaspoon garlic salt
Vegetable oil for frying

Rinse blossoms and strip off green portions on outside of flowers. Mix milk, egg, flour, cornmeal, and garlic salt in shallow pan. Heat ½ inch of oil in small frying pan. Dip blossoms one at a time into batter. Fry over medium heat, turning until golden brown on all sides.

Stuffed Blossoms

Makes Two Dozen

¼ cup green onions, chopped
1 clove garlic, minced
2 tablespoons oil
½ cup riccota cheese or tofu
⅓ cup grated Parmesan
  cheese
2 tablespoons chopped green
  chiles

2 dozen squash or pumpkin
  blossoms, 3 to 4 inches
  long
Flour
2 eggs
1 tablespoon water
Vegetable oil for frying

In frying pan sauté green onion and garlic in 2 tablespoons oil until limp. In a bowl combine ricotta cheese or crumbled tofu, Parmesan cheese, green chiles, and the cooked onion and garlic. Roughly divide filling and spoon a portion into each blossom. Twist tips to close. Roll each blossom in flour to lightly coat. In a small bowl, beat eggs with 1 tablespoon of water. Heat oil in small frying pan over medium high heat. Dip each stuffed and floured blossom into egg mixture and fry until golden brown. Drain on paper towels. Keep warm in oven until ready to serve.

Squash Blossom Soup

Serves Four to Six

2 to 2½ dozen pumpkin or
  squash blossoms
¼ cup chopped onion
1 clove garlic, minced

¼ cup butter or margarine
2 cups chicken broth .
2 cups whole milk
½ teaspoon salt

Rinse blossoms; remove and discard stems and other tough greenish portions. Chop blossoms coarsely. In frying pan cook onion and garlic in butter until limp, add chopped blossoms and sauté a few more minutes until they too are limp. Pour contents of skillet into a blender jar with one cup of the chicken broth and mix until smooth. In a deep saucepan, heat the blended mixture, the milk, and the remaining broth. Season with salt to taste.

Sundowner Soup

Serves Six

This recipe makes a hearty main dish soup that is special enough for company.

2 tablespoons margarine or
  oil
1 medium onion, chopped
2 garlic cloves, minced
1 can (16 ounces) hominy
1 teaspoon cumin
1½ quarts stock (chicken,
  vegetable, or bouillon
  cubes)
4 cups cooked, mashed,
  pumpkin or winter squash
Salt and pepper

Condiments:

6 tortillas
1 avocado
1½ cups grated Monterey
  jack or Mexican white
  cheese
4 medium tomatoes
3 green onions
3 tablespoons chopped
  canned green chiles
Garlic salt

Heat margarine or oil in small frying pan and sauté onion and garlic until transparent. Transfer to blender jar. Drain hominy, reserving liquid. Add hominy to blender jar with a little of the liquid and the cumin. Whirl until almost smooth (it will remain somewhat grainy). Add the rest of the hominy liquid and blend. In a large pot, combine hominy mixture, stock, and mashed pumpkin or squash. Stir until well blended. Add salt and pepper to taste.

Condiments: Cut tortillas into thin strips and fry in hot oil until crisp. Drain on paper towels. Coarsely chop avocado. Core and chop tomatoes. Slice onions. Combine tomatoes, onions, chopped green chiles and garlic salt to taste.

To serve: Place tortillas, avocado, grated cheese, and tomato salsa in separate bowls. Serve soup in bowls. At the table pass the condiments so guests can add what they wish to their soup.

Sour Cream Squash

Serves Four to Six

4 cups cubed, pared winter
  squash
1 medium onion
1 tablespoon butter

1 cup dairy sour cream
½ teaspoon salt
¼ teaspoon mace

Cook squash in a steamer over boiling water until very tender. Meanwhile, slice onion and cook in butter until limp but not brown. Remove from heat and stir in sour cream, salt, and mace.

Arrange hot cooked squash in shallow casserole. Pour the cream over the mixture.

Winter Squash Soufflé

Serves Six to Eight

2 pounds winter squash or
    pumpkin
¼ teaspoon dried thyme
2 tablespoons butter melted

2 tablespoons cream
Salt and pepper to taste
¼ cup grated Swiss cheese
3 eggs, separated

Peel and seed squash or pumpkin. Cut into pieces about 2 inches square and cook in a steamer until soft. Meanwhile, butter a two-quart baking dish. Preheat oven to 350 degrees F. In a medium bowl, beat egg whites until stiff and set aside. Transfer cooked squash to a large bowl and mash until it is a smooth puree. Mix in thyme, butter, cream, salt, and pepper to taste. Beat egg yolks and add them one at a time. Fold beaten egg whites into squash. Turn into buttered two-quart baking dish and bake in preheated oven for twenty to thirty minutes or until set and golden on top.

Winter Squash with Madeira

Serves Four to Six

1½ pounds winter squash or
    pumpkin
2½ tablespoons butter
2 tablespoons vegetable oil
Salt and pepper to taste
1 cup heavy cream

¼ cup Madeira or sherry
½ cup bread crumbs
½ cup walnuts or pecans
    coarsely chopped
2 tablespoons melted butter
Salt and pepper

Butter a one-quart baking dish. Preheat oven to 325 degrees F. Peel and seed squash or pumpkin. Cut into ¼-inch thick slices. Heat butter and vegetable oil in large frying pan over medium heat. Sauté squash slices in butter and oil until lightly browned. Place half the squash in prepared baking dish. Sprinkle with salt and pepper. Combine cream and Madeira in a bowl and pour half this mixture over the squash in the dish. Add remaining squash, then remaining cream. Combine bread crumbs and nuts with melted butter and sprinkle over top. Bake in preheated oven for forty-five minutes or until tender.

Squash and Tomatoes
Serves Two to Four

Gary Nabhan and his wife Karen Reichart taught me to make this dish using the hard-shell Cucurbita mixta *that grows so well in hot, dry climates. It has become a regular part of the menu at our house. When served over rice with a side of beans, it makes a complete meal. When I am living in a part of the world where it is difficult to get green chiles, I substitute green peppers.*

2 to 3 tablespoons oil
2 or 3 medium onions, cut
  in eighths
2 to 3 cups peeled squash,
  cut in 1-inch pieces

1 large can (24 ounces)
  tomatoes
1 can (4 ounces) chopped
  green chiles

Sauté onions in oil in covered frying pan. When slightly soft, add squash, green chiles, and tomatoes. Use spatula or spoon to break up tomatoes slightly. Cover pan and cook on low until squash is tender, fifteen to twenty minutes. If mixture is getting dry, add a little water; if too wet, cook uncovered for a few minutes to evaporate some of the liquid.

Pumpkin-Apple Butter

Makes Four Pints

1 3-pound pumpkin or squash
  (about 4 cups cooked)
5 apples
1¼ cups brown sugar
1¼ cups granulated sugar

2 tablespoons grated
  lemon peel
½ cup lemon juice
1 tablespoon pumpkin
  pie spice

Sterilize four pint jars and lids by boiling for fifteen minutes. Peel and cut pumpkin into small chunks. Place chunks in a large kettle with a small amount of water or pile chunks in a steamer. Cook pumpkin, covered for twenty to thirty minutes or until very tender. Drain off water and crush with a potato masher or whirl in a blender or food processor until smooth.

While pumpkin is cooking, quarter and core apples (unpeeled). Cut in large chunks and simmer or steam until soft. Whirl in a blender until pureed.

Combine pumpkin, apple, brown and white sugars, lemon peel, lemon juice, and spice and cook, stirring, over medium heat until sugar is dissolved. Reduce heat and simmer, stirring often to prevent sticking, for thirty to forty minutes or until mixture is thick. Pack in sterile jars.

Pumpkin Chips

This recipe will compete with any potato chip ever produced.

Fresh pumpkin or winter
  squash

Vegetable oil

Pare pumpkin or squash, taking away as little flesh as possible. Slice as thinly as you can so that you have pieces as wide as the wall of the vegetable and 2 to 4 inches long. Soak slices in water for one hour. Pat dry with paper towels. Heat oil to 360 degrees F. and try a few slices at a time until lightly browned. Drain. Sprinkle with salt, garlic salt, a mixture of curry powder and salt, or one of the herbal salt-substitutes.

Pumpkin Pancakes

Serves Four

This recipe, which originates in South Africa, makes a good luncheon dish when served with chutney and yogurt.

1½ cups peeled pumpkin or winter squash, cut in 1-inch cubes
1 egg, lightly beaten
½ cup sifted flour

⅛ teaspoon baking soda
1 tablespoon cinnamon
Vegetable oil for frying
½ cup sugar

Cook pumpkin in a steamer over boiling water until very tender. Transfer to a medium bowl and mash to a smooth puree. Add beaten egg and combine. Slowly stir in flour and soda, mixing well. Stir together sugar and cinnamon and set aside.

Heat ½ inch of oil in a large heavy skillet over high heat. Drop about 2 tablespoons of batter into the hot oil for each pancake and brown on both sides, turning once. Drain on paper towels and sprinkle with the cinnamon sugar mixture. Makes about sixteen pancakes.

Pumpkin Waffles

Makes Eight to Ten Waffles

Try these for a late Sunday breakfast some wintery morning while you are curled in front of the fireplace with the newspaper.

2½ cups sifted flour
4 teaspoons baking powder
1 tablespoon sugar
1 teaspoon salt
¾ teaspoon cinnamon
½ teaspoon nutmeg

3 eggs separated
1¾ cups milk
½ cup vegetable oil
½ cup pumpkin puree
¾ cup chopped pecans

Sift dry ingredients together in large bowl. In medium bowl, beat egg yolks; add milk, oil, and pumpkin. Add wet ingredients to dry ingredients and stir to combine.

Beat egg whites until stiff. Gently fold into batter. Heat waffle iron. Pour batter onto hot griddle, sprinkle with a few chopped pecans, and bake according to manufacturer's instructions.

Variation: Substitute 2 to 4 tablespoons of sesame oil for part of the vegetable oil and use ½ cup sesame seed instead of pecans. Makes a crisp and delicious waffle.

Pumpkin Cookies

Makes Nine Dozen

2 cups shortening
2 cups sugar
2 eggs
2 cups cooked mashed
  pumpkin
2 teaspoons vanilla
4 cups flour

2 teaspoons baking soda
2 teaspoons baking powder
1 teaspoon salt
2 teaspoons cinnamon
2 cups raisins
1 cup chopped nuts

Lightly grease a baking sheet. Preheat oven to 350 degrees F. In a large bowl, cream shortening and sugar until fluffy. Add eggs and pumpkin, blending well. Add vanilla. Beat in flour, baking soda, baking powder, salt, and cinnamon. Stir in raisins and nuts.

Drop by teaspoonfuls onto greased baking sheet and bake in preheated oven for ten to twelve minutes.

Pumpkin Cheesecake

Serves Ten to Twelve

The ginger cookie crust for which directions are given here is very tasty, but for variety you might try Mesquite Pie Crust (page 73) or any crumb crust of your choosing.

6 tablespoons butter or margarine	1 teaspoon ground cinnamon
2 cups finely crushed ginger cookies	½ teaspoon ginger
	½ teaspoon nutmeg
1 package (8 ounces) cream cheese	¼ teaspoon allspice
	3 eggs
¾ cup sugar	1 cup sour cream
2 tablespoons flour	2 tablespoons sugar
2 cups pumpkin puree	1 teaspoon vanilla

Preheat oven to 350 degrees F. Melt butter or margarine and blend with cookie crumbs. Pat in the bottom of an ungreased 9-inch square pan. Bake ten minutes in preheated oven. Cool.

In a large bowl, beat cream cheese, sugar, and flour until mixture is creamy. Add pumpkin, spices, and eggs and beat until smooth and well combined. Pour into crust and return to 350 degree F. oven for one hour or until knife inserted in center comes out clean.

Combine sour cream, 2 tablespoons sugar, and vanilla and spread over top of warm cake. Refrigerate at least four hours.

Pumpkin Spice Cake

Serves Sixteen

One Thanksgiving some friends and I took a holiday camping trip along the coastline of northern Sonora, Mexico. We took along a complete Thanksgiving dinner and I packed this cake, thinking it would travel better than pie. We ate our dinner watching the moon rise over the beautiful Sea of Cortez, and we were very thankful for all our blessings.

2½ cups sifted flour
1 teaspoon baking powder
1 teaspoon soda
1 teaspoon salt
¾ teaspoon cinnamon
¾ teaspoon cloves
¾ cup granulated sugar

½ cup brown sugar
¾ cup shortening
½ cup buttermilk
1½ cups mashed, cooked pumpkin
3 eggs
Whipped cream or substitute

Preheat oven to 350 degrees F. Grease and flour two 8-inch square pans or one larger pan. Sift together flour, baking powder, soda, salt, cinnamon, cloves, and granulated sugar in a large bowl. Add brown sugar, shortening, buttermilk, and pumpkin and beat two minutes. Add eggs and beat two minutes longer. Turn batter into prepared cake pans. Bake for thirty to thirty-five minutes (longer for the larger cake). At home, serve with real whipped cream. If you are camping, you will have to resort to pressurized cream or powdered whipped topping mix.

Harvest Ice Cream

Makes One Quart

1 cup mashed, cooked pumpkin or winter squash
½ cup brown sugar
¼ teaspoon pumpkin pie spice

½ teaspoon grated orange peel
3 tablespoons sherry
1 cup whipping cream

In a large bowl, combine all ingredients except whipping cream and stir until sugar is dissolved. Pour into bread pan and freeze for one hour. Meanwhile, chill whipping cream, bowl, and electric beaters or wire wisk in refrigerator. When pumpkin mixture is firm but not hard, whip cream. Fold whipped cream and pumpkin mixture together until well blended. Return to bread pan and freeze.

Flan de Calabaza

Serves Eight

Use a spoon with a very long handle to stir this. It sputters as it boils and can burn your hand.

1 cup white sugar	1½ cups water
3 cups mashed, cooked pumpkin or squash	2 teaspoons cinnamon
	½ cup all-purpose flour
1 can (12 ounces) evaporated milk	¾ cup brown sugar
	1 tablespoon vanilla

Place white sugar in a heavy skillet over medium heat and shake and stir with a wooden spatula until the sugar turns liquid and brown. Working quickly, pour the syrup into the bottom of a flat two-quart serving dish and tilt the dish so the syrup runs to cover the entire bottom. Set aside.

Combine pumpkin, evaporated milk, sugar, cinnamon, and 1 cup of the water in a large saucepan. In a jar with a tight fitting lid, mix ½ cup water and the flour and shake to combine. Add to the pumpkin mixture. Cook over low heat, stirring constantly, in a figure-eight pattern until the mixture is so thick that a spoonful scooped up and gently placed on top of the rest retains its shape.

Pour pumpkin into the prepared serving dish and cool. Mixture will thicken more as it cools and caramel will melt. Serve chilled or at room temperature.

SUNFLOWERS

Ah sunflower! weary of time
Who countest the steps of the sun
Seeking after that sweet golden clime
Where the traveler's journey is done.

WILLIAM BLAKE
Songs of Experience, 1794

William Blake's poem is based on a commonly held belief that sunflowers follow the sun with their heads. Botanists tell us that all green plants are slightly phototropic (growing toward the sun), and sunflowers are even more so, but they do not actually follow the sun through the day. It is, however, not unusual to pass a field of sunflowers and find all the flowers are facing in the same direction, and this fact, no doubt, gave rise to the belief.

When Europeans first arrived on the North American continent, they were struck by the fields of yellow flowers, a kind they had never before seen. They were even more amazed by the giant variety cultivated by the Indians who used the seeds for food.

The Europeans carried the seeds back home and there the plant became a common garden flower. Linneaus, the great taxonomist, gave it the genus name of *Helianthus* from the Greek *helios* meaning sun and *anthos* meaning flower. There are now sixty-seven species of sunflowers, most of them confined to North America.

Sunflower

As white civilization spread on our continent and a variety of horticultural plants became available, the sunflower became less important as a food, but when it spread into Russia from Eastern Europe, it boomed. Botanist Charles Heiser, in his book *The Sunflower*, tells why:

The Holy Orthodox Church of Russia in the early 19th century observed very strict regulations governing the diet of the people during the 40 days of Lent and the 40 days preceding Christmas. A number of foods including nearly all foods rich in oil were prohibited during these periods, but the sunflower, which had only recently entered the country was not on the list. The people eagerly adopted it, for it was a source of oil and could be eaten without breaking the letter of the law. As a result of this, the popularity of the sunflower became immense.

Then, in the early twentieth century, a Russian agronomist developed a sunflower with almost twice as much oil as standard varieties. Soon the sunflower was the prime source of edible oil in Russia. Its reputation spread, the plant was reestablished in the United States, and now sunflowers are the second most important world oil crop after soybeans. In the United States sunflower acreage doubled in the 1970s.

Large-seeded giant sunflowers are growing in popularity as a snack food in our country and are appearing in granola cereals and in snack packs in local grocery stores. The availability of the shelled kernels is also appealing to consumers.

While these products will no doubt continue to grow in popularity, the real food of the future is sunflower meal which is left over after sunflower oil is extracted. Currently most of it is being fed to cattle, but with the need for human protein sources, we cannot ignore this resource much longer.

Sunflower meal has about 47 percent protein, more than soybean meal. It is low in lysine, but that can be offset by combining sunflower meal with legumes, which are usually high in lysine. Two other drawbacks to mass marketing of sunflower meal are the grayish color of the meal, a rather unappetizing hue, and the high fiber content which some people find difficult to digest. Several university programs are currently studying methods of isolating sunflower protein to get around these problems.

There are also other sunflower by-products. In Canada the hulls are pressed into logs for burning. The Soviets use the hulls in manufacturing ethyl alcohol, in lining plywood, and in growing yeast, while the pithy stems are incorporated into lightweight acoustical ceiling tile.

Sunflower Meal

Although commercial sunflower meal has had the oil removed, meal made at home contains the sunflower oil as well as the protein. The simplest way to make it is to whirl about a quarter cup of hulled sunflower kernels in a blender until they are ground fine. Grain grinders and meat grinders also work well. In each case, use the finest blade.

The first three recipes below call for sunflower meal.

Sunflower Orange Rolls

Makes Eighteen

Dough:

1 package active dry yeast
½ cup warm water
¾ cup milk, scalded
   and cooled
2 tablespoons honey
1 egg
½ teaspoon salt
2 tablespoons vegetable oil
3½ to 4½ cups unbleached
   flour

Filling:

1 cup sunflower meal
   (page 188)
1 cup brown sugar
½ teaspoon nutmeg
½ teaspoon cinnamon
½ teaspoon vanilla
1 egg
2 tablespoons grated orange
   peel
¼ cup sunflower seeds

In a large bowl, dissolve yeast in warm water. Stir in scalded milk, honey, salt, egg, oil, and 2 cups of the flour. Beat until smooth. Mix in enough remaining flour to make a soft dough. Knead until smooth and elastic. Turn into a greased bowl and let rise until doubled. Punch dough down and roll into a rectangle about 14×18 inches. Mix filling ingredients and spread on dough. Starting with long edge, roll up. Slice into 1-inch thick rolls and place on greased cookie sheets. Let rise again until doubled. Bake at 375 degrees F. for twenty minutes or until golden brown. Frost with orange glaze (powdered sugar and orange juice) if desired.

Rich Sunflower Spread

Melt-in-your-mouth rich, this spread will be a party favorite when molded into a half sphere, garnished with chopped black olives and parsley, and surrounded by good crackers. Any leftovers can be used as a lunchbox spread on whole wheat bread, layered with sliced tomatoes and alfalfa sprouts.

⅓ pound tofu
¼ cup sunflower meal
  (page 188)
1 tablespoon sesame tahini
  (or peanut butter)

2 tablespoons mayonnaise
2 tablespoons lemon juice
Sprinkle of garlic powder

Mash tofu with a fork until crumbly. Add remaining ingredients, stirring until well blended.

Zuni Sunflower Pudding

Serves Six to Eight

This pudding is delicious and easy. Fresh corn is best but frozen can be substituted.

1 cup fresh corn kernels
1 cup sunflower meal
  (page 188)
1 cup finely chopped summer
  squash

2 cups water
1 teaspoon salt

Grind corn kernels in blender until fairly liquid. Combine with sunflower meal, squash, water, and salt in a heavy covered saucepan. Simmer over very low heat for forty-five minutes, stirring occasionally. If mixture is not yet thick, uncover pan and continue cooking, watching carefully lest the pudding stick and burn as it thickens. Delicious warm or cold.

Variation: Near the end of the cooking, add 2 to 4 tablespoons chopped green chiles.

Sunny Green Beans
Serves Four

2 cups sliced green beans
½ cup chopped green onion
¼ cup sunflower seeds

2 tablespoons oil
1 to 2 tablespoons soy sauce

In a medium pot over boiling water, steam the green beans until just tender. Heat oil in a small frying pan and sauté the onion in the oil until golden brown. Add the sunflower seeds and stir. In serving bowl, toss the green beans with the onion and sunflower seed mixture. Season to taste with soy sauce.

Sunflower Seed Cookies
Makes Three Dozen

1 cup brown sugar
¾ cup margarine
1 egg
1 teaspoon vanilla
1½ cups whole wheat flour
¾ cup wheat germ

1½ teaspoons baking powder
¾ teaspoon salt
1 teaspoon cinnamon
½ cup flaked coconut
½ cup chopped dates
½ cup sunflower seeds

In a large bowl beat brown sugar and margarine together until creamy. Add egg and vanilla and beat.

Combine flour, wheat germ, baking powder, salt, cinnamon, and coconut. Stir this mixture into the wet mixture, along with the dates and sunflower seeds.

Drop dough by heaping teaspoonfuls about 2 inches apart on lightly greased baking sheets. Bake in a 350 degree F oven for ten to twelve minutes or until golden. Cool on brown paper or racks.

Sunflower Rolled Waffles
Makes Ten

This recipe is reprinted from Recipes for a Small Planet *(Ballantine Books) with the permission of author Ellen Buchman Ewald, who has carefully balanced the ingredients to provide for the greatest complement of proteins. Each waffle provides 16 to 19 percent of the average daily protein needs of an adult.*

1 cup rolled oats
1 cup rolled wheat
2 cups hot water
6 tablespoons non-instant
  milk powder
  (½ cup instant)

1 egg, beaten
2 tablespoons oil
2 tablespoons honey
¼ teaspoon salt
⅔ cup sunflower seeds
2 teaspoons baking powder

Put the oats and wheat into a small mixing bowl. Pour the hot water over them and stir. Let the mixture sit and soften for a few minutes. Add the remaining ingredients in the order given, stirring carefully after each addition.

To bake, spread about ½ cup batter over a hot, oiled waffle iron. Use a wooden spoon to spread the batter almost to the edge (as this batter does not spread like thin waffle batters).

Bake until very brown and crisp. Serve with yogurt, apple sauce and cinnamon, or syrup and butter.

Apricot Sun Balls

Makes Four Dozen

These are great for stuffing into a backpack to eat after dinner sitting around a campfire. Also good at home for after-school treats.

2 oranges	1 cup chopped sunflower
1 pound dried apricots	seeds
6 tablespoons honey	1 cup flaked coconut

Grate the rind of one of the oranges. Juice both oranges. Put the apricots through a food grinder. In a heavy saucepan, combine all ingredients except the seeds and the coconut. Cook ten minutes, stirring constantly to avoid burning. Add chopped sunflower seeds and stir. Cool and shape into small balls. It helps to butter your fingers a little. Roll balls in coconut. Store in refrigerator.

Foods of the
Future

BUFFALO GOURD

To the uninitiated there could hardly be a less likely candidate for a new food plant than the buffalo gourd (*Cucurbita foetidissima*). This viney plant, which is found growing widely throughout the West along roadsides and in abandoned fields up to 7000 feet in elevation, would strike few people as an acceptable dish for supper. The plant has rough sticky leaves, an odd odor, and hard, dry, tennis ball-sized fruits which taste so bitter they can curl your tongue and send a shiver from your neck to your heels.

But this wild weedy relative of the pumpkin is a Cinderella plant: strip away the bitter pulp of the fruits and crack the hulls off the 300-odd seeds inside and you find a seed embryo that is 37 percent high quality protein and one-half edible oil. After the oil has been expressed from the seed, the remaining residue has about 50 percent protein. What is more, hidden beneath the soil under every plant is a large storage root which can be processed to produce a fine starch similar to corn starch. The buffalo gourd is a perennial plant and every year the root grows and branches; in exceptional cases they can weigh a hundred pounds and be as tall as a man.

Buffalo gourd seeds are inevitably compared to soybeans and in many ways, the gourd seeds come out ahead. The two seeds are similar in protein content, both being low in the sulphur amino acids methionine and cystine and borderline in lysine.

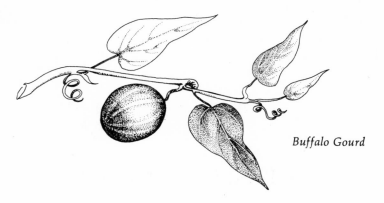

Buffalo Gourd

The two crops produce roughly the same net amount of food value per acre.

Buffalo gourd oil, however, tends to go rancid less quickly than soybean oil, and buffalo gourd seeds have fewer flatulent sugars (those little devils that sometimes make beans a socially difficult food) than soybeans. On the minus side, commercially produced buffalo gourd oil is dark and seems resistant to bleaching although it has recently been discovered that oil that is hand expressed has none of the objectionable coloration.

The buffalo gourd has been the subject of investigations at the University of Arizona and in the Middle East since the early 1960s and a group of researchers in Australia have begun a 100-acre pilot project in northern Queensland. Once the plant has been thoroughly researched there are plans to attempt to introduce it into extremely arid regions of the world such as the Sahel in West Africa where the populations desperately need crops which will produce nutritious food on very limited water. Tests have shown that after the plants are established they will thrive with once-a-month irrigation although because of the large storage root they will *live* without water for up to a year.

The future of the buffalo gourd as food will be largely in terms of commercially prepared products. However, if you wish to get ahead of the crowd, you can follow these steps to prepare the seeds for use in the recipe for Gourdola Bars.

Collect the gourds in the fall when they are dry and yellow.

Separate the seeds from the dry pulp. Tie the seeds in an old pillowcase or a washed flour sack and send them through an automatic washer without any soap. It is very difficult to extract the seed embryos from the seed coats by hand (and you probably do not own a commercial seed decorticator) so just use the whole seeds. They will be crunchy and full of fiber but they will not hurt you.

Gourdola Bars

Makes Thirty Pieces

This recipe is adapted from one developed by Carol Coles for a University of Arizona research project involving possible uses of buffalo gourd seeds.

½ cup oatmeal	*Syrup:*
2 tablespoons nonfat dry milk	¾ cup brown sugar
1⅓ cups buffalo gourd seeds	¾ cup white sugar
¼ cup sesame seeds	½ cup corn syrup
¼ cup sunflower seeds	½ cup water
1 cup raw peanuts	1 teaspoon vinegar
½ cup almonds finely chopped	¼ teaspoon salt
1 cup raisins	¾ cup margarine
20 dates, chopped to about	2 tablespoons cinnamon
six pieces per date	1 tablespoon ginger

In a large bowl, combine oatmeal, dry milk, seeds, nuts, and fruit; mix well. Set aside. To make the syrup, combine the sugars, corn syrup, water, vinegar, and salt and heat in a quart saucepan over medium to high heat until the temperature of the mixture reaches about 275 degrees F. (soft crack stage) on a candy thermometer. Turn off the heat and add the margarine, mixing well until it is incorporated and the mixture is thicker. Add the cinnamon and ginger and mix well.

Pour this mixture slowly in a thin stream over the granola

mixture, stirring well so that all of the dry ingredients are coated. Shape handfuls into rolls of one-inch diameter and slice into two-inch pieces. To store, wrap tightly in plastic wrap and keep at room temperature.

CATTAILS

An aquatic plant such as the cattail might seem a strange choice for inclusion in a book devoted to foods indigenous to the dry Southwest, but this hardy plant is as widespread as some cactus. It will grow in irrigation ditches and in lakes so small they would be called ponds in any other part of the country.

Southwestern Indians have been gathering and eating parts of the cattail for centuries. In clearly documented studies, anthropologists tell us that the Paiute of Humbolt Sink in Nevada relied on cattail seeds as food for more than a thousand years while occupying Lovelock Cave between A.D. 750 and 1800.

Today the fine art of cattail stalking is still alive in parts of Europe as well as here at home, although the sport unfortunately is restricted to those lucky few who have learned the basics from a friend or relative or perhaps have stumbled upon the secret in a book or magazine article.

As the world grows hungrier and the supply of perfectly adapted farm acreage grows smaller, however, the *cognoscenti* will probably have to give up their exclusive rights to this delicacy, for the various parts of the cattail are nutritious additions to any diet.

The cattail gathering season begins in the early spring when the roots which have lain dormant and buried in mud for the cold season begin to send out shoots which will eventually become graceful long leaves. The shoots are white or pale green and very

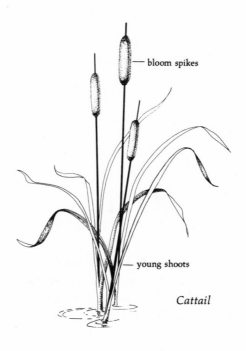

bloom spikes

young shoots

Cattail

crisp. Reportedly popular in western Russia, these shoots are sometimes called Cossack asparagus. The fresh-tasting leaves, which are layered much like a leek, can be gathered, chopped into inch-long pieces, steamed, and buttered for a simple dish or included in Cossack Salad if you are interested in a slightly more complex recipe.

The next delicacy that this generous plant offers for our tables is the bloom stalk with its unusual sausage-shaped flower heads, arranged one above the other. While these bloom spikes are still green and tightly closed, they can be cut apart (so that each looks like a hot dog with a knitting needle stuck through it the long way), and steamed for about fifteen minutes. When they are tender you can eat them with butter like corn on the cob. The green buds can also be cut from the stalk and included in the recipe for Cattail Bud Pilaf.

In the late spring in the lower desert, or mid to late summer at higher elevations, the upper portion of the cattail bloom spike begins to take on an amber blush and soon becomes gloriously golden with rich pollen. This pollen can be easily gathered by bending the flexible stalks into a paper bag and shaking vigorously to release the pollen. The pollen can be substituted for a portion of the flour in any of your favorite recipes for baked goods or used in one of the recipes given here.

Perhaps the most nutritious part of the cattail is the thick root or rhizome, which is rich in carbohydrates. Although the method of producing flour from these roots is not beyond the skills of an average ten- to twelve-year-old, it is a messy, time-consuming project. (Full instructions are given in my book *American Indian Food and Lore*.) However, simple processing machinery could easily handle the task of producing flour in commercial quantities.

Several years ago two scientists working at Syracuse University investigated the possibilities of growing cattails commercially. Their research showed that they could harvest 140 tons of cattail rhizomes per acre which could be processed into thirty-two tons of flour, a yield in food value far ahead of other staples such as potatoes, wheat, rye, oats, millet, or maize.

Cattail gathering is a good task for older children who grow bored during a family outing to a fresh-water fishing spot. Cattails cannot be confused with anything poisonous and are so easy to gather that they give a quick sense of accomplishment. It is also a good way to introduce children to what may become a common food of the twenty-first century.

Cossack Salad

Serves Six

This recipe is adapted from one I found in Gourmet Magazine. *The author, Paul Kinslow, prefaced his recipes with a
humorous tale of being stopped during a fishing trip by a
suspicious game warden who eyed his bulging creel and warned
him that legally he was allowed only eight trout. Imagine the
warden's surprise when a peek in the creel revealed not trout but
cattails.*

*For this recipe, pick the cattail shoots when they are ten to
twelve inches long. You might have to reach under the water to
get a firm grasp so that the shoot will detach at the root;
otherwise, you risk ending up with just a handful of outer
leaves.*

24 young cattail shoots
1 cup plain yogurt
½ cup mayonnaise
1 tablespoon minced fresh
    chives
Sprinkle of garlic powder
1½ teaspoons minced fresh
    or ½ teaspoon dried basil

Salt to taste
Dash white pepper
1 head Boston or other soft
    lettuce
¼ cup chopped fresh parsley

Trim off and discard the green tops of the cattails, reserving
the lower three inches of each shoot. Peel off and discard the
outer layers of the reserved shoots to expose the ivory-colored
inner stalks. Cut the shoots crosswise into one-inch sections.
Over boiling water, steam the shoots for five to ten minutes until
crisp-tender.

Meanwhile, in a medium bowl, combine the yogurt, mayonnaise, chives, herbs, and spices.

When shoots are cooked tender, combine in a bowl with part
or all of the dressing (to your taste). Chill for about an hour.

When ready to serve, arrange lettuce on six salad plates. Pile shoots on top of lettuce and sprinkle with fresh parsley. A slice of fresh red tomato and perhaps a black olive will add color to the plate.

Cattail Bud Pilaf

Serves Six to Eight

The measurement of cattail buds in this recipe is not critical; if you arrive home with more or less, use what you have.

¼ cup chopped onions
¼ cup vegetable oil
2 cups fresh green cattail buds scraped from bloom spikes
1 egg
2 tablespoons water

2 cups cooked rice or bulgur wheat
¼ cup nutmeats or sunflower kernels
Salt and pepper to taste

In a large heavy frying pan, heat oil; sauté the onions until transparent; then add the cattail buds and sauté until tender, about ten minutes. Meanwhile, mix the egg with the water and beat. In another frying pan coated with just enough oil or butter to prevent sticking, fry the egg mixture into a large thin pancake. When dry and slightly brown, turn out onto a cutting board. With a sharp knife, slice into thin slivers.

Add the rice or bulgur to the cattail mixture and combine. Gently add the egg strips and heat through. Add the nutmeats or sunflower kernels and season to taste. Serve hot.

Golden Crepes

Makes One Dozen

By the addition of salt or sugar these delicious crepes can serve either as a main dish or a dessert.

½ cup cattail pollen
½ cup all-purpose flour
1 egg, beaten
⅔ cup milk

Sprinkle of salt or
  2 teaspoons sugar
1 teaspoon melted butter
Oil for frying

Combine all ingredients in a large bowl using either the salt or sugar. Let the batter sit in the refrigerator for thirty minutes to an hour before making the crepes.

Stir batter well before using. Heat a 7- or 8-inch crepe pan over medium-high heat and brush lightly with oil. Pour in about 3 tablespoons of batter, quickly tilting pan to spread batter evenly. As edge begins to dry, loosen with a metal spatula. When brown on bottom, turn and lightly brown other side. Slip onto a clean towel.

Variations: For main dish crepes, chop and steam about 3 cups of mixed vegetables. Meanwhile make 3 cups of medium white sauce seasoned with some grated Parmesan cheese, a little sherry, and perhaps one of your favorite herbs. When the vegetables are very tender, mix enough of the white sauce with them to bind. Fill each crepe with ¼ cup of the mixture, roll, and place seam side down on a serving plate. When all crepes are filled, pour the remaining sauce over them and slide under the broiler until hot and bubbly.

For dessert crepes, melt ½ cup apricot preserves with ¼ cup orange juice mixed with 1 teaspoon of cornstarch. Spread each crepe with 1 tablespoon of the mixture, fold into quarters, and place slightly overlapping on a shallow greased baking pan. Dot with butter and bake at 350 degrees F. for five or ten minutes. To serve, place two crepes on a dessert plate and top with a dollop of whipped cream or a small scoop of vanilla ice cream.

Cattail Carrot Cake

Serves Ten to Twelve

The day after I collected cattail pollen was my father's birthday. I concocted this recipe for a rich, festive-looking cake that needs no frosting.

½ cup cattail pollen
1 cup flour
1 cup sugar
1 teaspoon baking powder
1 teaspoon salt
1 teaspoon cinnamon

½ teaspoon soda
⅔ cup salad oil
2 eggs
1 cup grated carrots
½ cup crushed pineapple
1 teaspoon vanilla

Sift together dry ingredients. Add oil, eggs, grated carrot, pineapple, and vanilla and beat. Spread into a greased 8-inch or 9-inch square pan and bake at 350 degrees F. for thirty-five to forty minutes. Cool and cut into squares.

JOJOBA

Jojoba beans grow on a rather inconspicuous, tough-leaved grey-green bush, but these beans and the growing conditions of the bush that produces them have been the object of one of the most exciting international experiments in plant domestication in recent history.

The oil, or more accurately, liquid wax, from the jojoba (pronounced ho-ho-ba) bean has emerged in the past decade as a wonder lubricant that is used in cosmetics, paper coatings, electrical insulation, carbon paper, textiles, leather, pharmaceuticals, and polishes.

As a lubricant, jojoba oil is a replacement for sperm whale oil because it is resistant to friction and can tolerate high temperatures without breaking down. It is especially good for cosmetics because creams using the substance disappear into the skin rapidly and keep the skin supple amd smooth.

Until now most of the firms using jojoba oil have had to rely on supplies of jojoba beans gathered from wild bushes. Because it takes a thousand pounds of beans to make one 42-gallon barrel of oil, the price is high—in the neighborhood of $10,000.

Entrepreneurs have been quick to see the possibilities for profit in growing a plant which can survive on only eight to fourteen inches of rainfall and still produce a valuable product. The wave of excitement surrounding jojoba has led to the planting of more than 24,000 acres of jojoba bushes in Arizona and southern California and more in the Middle East.

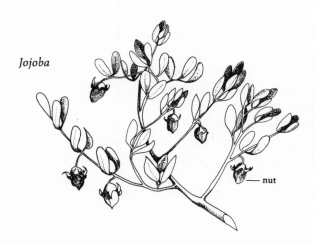

Jojoba

— nut

The experiments have not been without problems, however. For one thing, only female plants produce beans. Young plants have the uni-sex look, and growers have not been able to tell until plants are about four years old which will be the producers. Fortunately, a team of University of Arizona plant researchers have recently developed a method of cloning jojoba cuttings so that from now on jojoba farmers will be spared the expense of nurturing plants for years before discovering that they are unproductive males.

Because jojoba oil is slow to go rancid and can withstand high temperatures, it might make a good cooking oil, especially for industrial situations such as potato chip production where the fat is repeatedly subjected to high heat. Jojoba oil, however, will not find such widespread use until the price can be brought down. This means that uses will have to be found for the residue left behind after the oil has been expressed from the beans. There is already a highly developed technology in the utilization of other defatted oil seeds such as peanuts, cottonseed, soybeans, and sunflower seeds, but jojoba seed has not fit into the scheme without modifications. Although the residues are high in protein, other factors present in the untreated meal have made it so unpalatable to cattle that they would rather starve than eat it.

Hundreds of researchers worldwide are working to overcome the problems and are making remarkable progress. A method has been developed to extract protein concentrates from the defatted meal which eliminates the objectionable factors. While this product is too expensive to be fed to animals, it might be used like soy products as a fortifier and conditioner in commercial baked goods, meat products, and packaged whipped dessert mixes.

Southwestern Indians used jojoba beans for medicinal purposes and ate them occasionally as a snack. There is a slight bitter flavor from the tannins present in the beans; this and some other compounds could affect the health of anyone who ate them in quantity over a period of time, but most people suffer no ill effects from consuming a small number of jojoba beans such as might be present in a cup of jojoba beverage.

An easy method for preparing a handful or two of jojoba nuts for munching is to slip off the outer skins and spread the beans on a shallow pan or in a heavy frying pan. Roast them in a slow (250 degree F.) oven for about an hour, stirring occasionally. When they are done, put them in a bowl and sprinkle a tiny bit of mild-flavored vegetable oil over them. Add salt to taste.

Jojolate

Makes One Cup

This is by far the best jojoba bean concoction I have ever tasted. It is the invention of Dale Parra of Todos Santos, Baja California (you can read more about her and her interesting desert life in the Barrel Cactus section). Prepare the jojoba meal by roasting jojoba beans for one hour in a 250 degree F. oven or toasting them in a heavy frying pan stirring constantly over medium heat for ten to fifteen minutes. Grind as fine as possible in a blender, electric coffee mill or hand coffee grinder.

½ cup evaporated milk
½ cup water
1 tablespoon sugar

⅛ teaspoon cinnamon
3 tablespoons jojoba meal

Mix the milk and water and heat until almost boiling. Mix the sugar and cinnamon and add to the milk. Add a little of the milk mixture to the jojoba meal to make a thin paste, then add to the remaining milk. Heat, strain, and serve.

Note: Drinking a couple of cups of this beverage will do the average person no harm. If you tend to be sensitive to certain foods, however, or like it so much you want to make it a regular part of your diet, you can remove some of the toxins by a simple process developed by Ann Glenn Cotgageorge, a graduate student researcher. After you grind the whole roasted beans in a blender or mill, soak meal in water for six hours. Drain, spread on a cookie sheet, and when dry proceed as usual.

Jojoba Soap

Jojoba oil is available by the ounce in many specialty stores which sell fancy soaps, oils, and bath products. The following recipe is adapted from one developed by Anna Elias-Cesnick while she was editor of a publication called "Jojoba Happenings." The proportion of jojoba oil may be increased; for the vegetable oil, use your choice of peanut, corn, coconut, safflower, or a combination.

As you work use only ceramic, enamel, porcelain, stainless steel, or wooden utensils; lye will corrode iron, aluminum, tin, and nonstick fluorocarbon (Teflon, Silverstone) finishes. Lye is caustic, so wear rubber gloves whenever you are handling the materials. You will need a candy thermometer.

From the day you start making the soap until the time it is ready to use will be about a month; if you plan on using the soap for Christmas presents, start in November.

The soap can be colored with vegetable colors or spices—try tumeric for dark orange or powdered clove for a dark brown color and a wonderful scent. For other scents, use only essential oils. Anything with alcohol will cause the soap to separate.

2 heaping tablespoons lye
½ cup cold distilled water
2 tablespoons jojoba oil

6 tablespoons vegetable oil
½ cup rendered beef tallow
(directions given below)

In a small bowl, dissolve lye in the distilled water. (If you get lye on your skin, rinse immediately with vinegar.) In a heavy saucepan, heat fat and oils until they are about 95 to 98 degrees F. Turn off heat. When lye solution has cooled to the same temperature, put on rubber gloves and carefully pour the lye solution into the fat in a slow steady stream, stirring constantly and evenly until the mixture turns milky. Continue stirring until the mixture thickens, anywhere from forty-five minutes to two hours. When the texture resembles pudding, add the essential oils, spices, and colorings. The soap is now ready to be poured into plastic molds (try small freezer containers) or other molds (not tin or aluminum) which have a pleasing shape and have been coated with shortening or Vaseline or lined with plastic wrap. Cover the molds so that the soap will cool slowly.

After about a day and a half, unmold the soap, using rubber gloves to protect your hands. Let it dry for about a week. By this time the soap will no longer be caustic and you can clean it up by scraping off the whitish layer and cutting it into bars or carving nice beveled corners. Let the soap harden for another two or three weeks before using.

To render beef tallow: For this recipe you will need a little less than a pound of clean beef fat. Anywhere from a day to a month before you want to make the soap, cut the fat into small chunks. Place in a pan, cover with water, and bring to a boil. Simmer, stirring occasionally, for about four hours until all the fat has melted. Strain the "soup" through a strainer lined with cheese cloth. Cool to room temperature and refrigerate. When it hardens clean off the grey residue beneath it and toss out the water. At this point you can wrap the fat in plastic film and hold it for up to a month until you are ready to make the soap.

HALOPHYTES

Most plants are rather fussy about their drinking water. If offered anything with more than 5,000 parts of salt per million parts of water, there is a good chance the average plant will die.

Halophytes (from the classical Greek for salt and plant—*halo* and *phyte*) are an unusual group of salt-tolerant plants, some of which can survive in salinities greater than seawater which contains 30,000 to 40,000 parts of salt per million parts of water. Scientists estimate that there may be more than a thousand halophytes worldwide—bushes, succulents, grasses, and trees.

Because salt build-up takes 200,000 to 300,000 acres of cropland out of production each year, it is of considerable importance to begin to identify halophytic plants that can serve as food for man and animals. Salt accumulation is an inevitable consequence of irrigation in arid lands. Already considerable portions of the agricultural land in California and the lower Rio Grande Valley, both major breadbaskets of the nation, have serious salinity problems.

Simply stated, halophytes deal with salts in three essential ways: (1) they exclude them at the roots using ultra-filtration mechanisms; (2) they isolate them and then excrete the excess; and (3) they increase their own water content, thereby diluting the salts to a tolerable level.

Scientists associated with the Environmental Research Laboratory in Tucson, Arizona, have searched worldwide for potentially useful halophytes. Interestingly, some of the most promis-

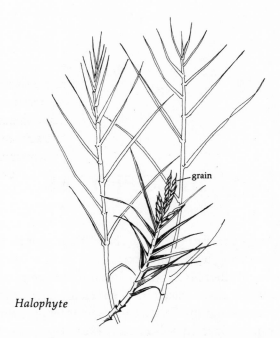

grain

Halophyte

ing were found in their own backyard—on the coast of the Gulf of California.

Palmer's saltgrass (*Distichlis palmeri*) was first described by Edward Palmer in 1885. The Cocopah Indians, living near the mouth of the Colorado River where it empties into the Gulf of California, cultivated an estimated 40,000 to 50,000 acres of the wheatlike grass. The plants were watered by the salty tidal waters. After Anglos moved to Arizona and California in greater numbers and began tampering with the flow of the Colorado River by means of upstream dams, the Cocopahs abandoned the cultivation of saltgrass, although a small wild population of the plant still exists on the northern reaches of the Gulf of California. Ed Glenn, Nick Yensen, and Miguel Fontes spent several years experimenting with methods of growing Palmer's saltgrass at the Environmental Research Laboratory.

Now, ecologist Yensen and his wife Susana Bojorquez de Yensen have focused their careers on the development of several saltgrass hybrids, which they are calling WildWheat. Their fields in northwest Mexico produced a ton of grain in 1986. It is most likely the first halophyte cereal crop to be cultivated using modern agricultural techniques.

It is an incredibly adaptable plant. Some types can grow in water up to one and a half times as salty as seawater; others can grow well at temperatures ranging from below freezing to 122 degrees Fahrenheit. One type can go for up to eight months without any water at all. Also, the grain is a perennial, meaning it does not require yearly planting, a great economic advantage.

The grain provides good nutrition as well. The fiber content of WildWheat is 8 percent compared to 3 percent for regular wheat. The protein level is slightly lower, but the mix of essential amino acids is well-balanced for a cereal crop. It contains no gluten, the principal cause of wheat allergies, and is low in phytates, substances that inhibit the body's absorption of certain vital minerals.

As detailed earlier in the book (page xv), the domestication and development of a new crop is a challenging process. Recognizing that a new food has the best chance of acceptance if it is associated with upscale living, the Yensens have marketed the grain through Neiman-Marcus and distributed it to gourmet restaurant chefs in Tucson.

Susana's scientific taste tests of muffins made with Wild-Wheat demonstrated that muffin consumers found little difference in the color, appearance, texture, or "mouthfeel" (more important than you might think) of muffins made with Wild-Wheat as compared to those made from regular whole wheat. The taste testers particularly liked the wholesome, nutty aroma of the WildWheat.

The Yensens hope that WildWheat can eventually be exported to Third World countries such as Pakistan, Sudan, Peru, and Chile, some of which have lost more than half of their agricultural land to salt build-up. The implications for the economies of these countries could be far-reaching depending on who controls the growing and distribution of the crop.

Another promising halophyte is pickleweed (*Salicornia europea*), a nutritious, succulent shrub which is a gourmet vegetable in Europe. A common plant along Mexico's arid coastlines, it is currently being field-tested in Mexico and in the Arabian Gulf coast sheikdom of Sharja in the United Arab Emirates. Even Mikhail Gorbachev, the Soviet leader, is interested in setting up *Salicornia* field trials along the coast of the Black Sea. Genesis, a Mexican corporation committed to commercializing halophytes, hopes that *Salicornia* may be one of a number of new developments which may help to revitalize the Mexican economy.

Of particular economic interest to all the developers are the *Salicornia* seeds. The plant produces more than 1.2 tons of seed per acre even when irrigated exclusively with seawater. The seed is 20 percent oil which can be refined into a high-quality edible oil similar to safflower oil. What remains of the seed after the oil is taken out is 43 percent protein. This seed meal and the green part of the plant both make excellent animal feed.

One unusual halophyte—eelgrass (*Zostera marina*)—grows as it floats in the ocean. The seeds of eelgrass were formerly an important traditional food source of the Seri Indians who live on the arid coastline of the Mexican state of Sonora. According to ethnobotanist Richard Felger, who learned about the plant from the Seri, eelgrass is ready to harvest in the month of April or early May. The protein and starch contents of the seed compare favorably with those of major economic grains grown on land, while the fat content is unusually low. The taste of the flour produced from the seed is bland. Although the Seri traditionally cook the flour into a sort of gruel, it can also be baked into bread.

Several researchers have combined their knowledge for the purpose of speculating on the possibility of growing these seagrasses on rafts, which would also have roosts for marine birds in order to provide fertilizer. Commercially significant fish might be attracted to the nutrient-rich water beneath the rafts. Their harvest and sale could offer a means to finance the long-term research and development for seagrass farming.

Other promising halophytes are a strange little cherry tomato which apparently escaped from cultivation and was found growing in water with 10 percent salinity; and some of the mesquites which are marginally salt-tolerant. Researchers also are working on salt-tolerant varieties of tepary beans, cowpeas, millet, barley, cotton, and alfalfa.

If these halophytes are accepted into the commercial markets or if new varieties of more familiar plants can be bred using some of the halophytes' salt-tolerant attributes, abundant supplies of saline water are available for arid land agriculture. These include saline aquifers that underlie millions of acres of desert, as well as unlimited ocean water to irrigate 20,000 miles of desert coastline.

Future advances are tied only to money and vision. Young scientists like the Yensens have the ideas, the skills, and the vision. Let us hope that they get the funding they need to help ensure that the populations of tomorrow can make use of these nutritious foods—foods the American Indians used for generations, foods that were lost to us and have only recently been rediscovered.

Susana's WildWheat Muffins
Makes One Dozen

1½ cups WildWheat flour	½ cup milk
2 teaspoons baking powder	½ cup honey
½ teaspoon salt	½ cup melted margarine
1 egg	

Preheat oven to 400 degrees F. Grease muffin cups or line with paper baking cups. In a large bowl, mix flour, baking powder, and salt. In a small bowl, beat egg with a fork; beat in milk, honey, and margarine. Add the wet mixture to the dry mixture, stirring until just blended. Fill prepared muffin cups two-thirds full. Bake in preheated oven for fifteen minutes or until golden brown.

Southwestern WildWheat Salad

Makes Four to Five Servings

Donna Nordin, executive chef at Tucson's popular Cafe Terra Cotta, developed this recipe.

½ cup (4 oz) raw WildWheat grain
3 cups water
½ cup cooked brown rice
⅔ cups cooked corn kernels
2 tablespoons lime juice
2 tablespoons olive oil
1 or 2 sliced green onions
1 or 2 cloves garlic, minced
¼ cup minced parsley
2 tablespoons minced cilantro (if desired)
½ cup sliced radishes (if desired)
Salt and pepper to taste
Lettuce leaves for garnish

In a large covered saucepan, cook WildWheat grain in 3 cups of water gently for fifty to sixty minutes. Drain off any excess water.

Mix cooked grain with remaining ingredients in a large serving bowl. Season with salt and pepper. Refrigerate at least two hours before serving. May be stored in the refrigerator for up to four days. Garnish with lettuce leaves when serving.

Reference Material

Reference Material

APPENDIX

Plants of the Southwest
The Railroad Yards
Santa Fe, NM 87501
This company offers blue corn, tomatillos, bolito beans, and native chiles. Send $1.00 for a catalog.

Redwood Seed Company
P.O. Box 361
Redwood City, CA 94064
Carries a variety of heirloom and wild seeds, particularly those adapted to California. Plant list is $.50.

Burpee Company
Warminster, PA 18974
This giant seed company carries seeds of tampala amaranth, but the catalog is so big you will have to search.

INDEX

Crosswhite, Frank, 26
Crunch Noodles, 37
Curcubita foetidissima, 197

Dad's Basic Beans, 145
Daniel, Stephanie, 32, 129
Desert Cake, 76
Desert Dawn Pie, 34
Desert Health Cereal, 39
Desert Jewel Pie, 10
The Desert Smells Like Rain
  (Nabhan), 28
Desserts. *See also* Cake; Candy;
  Cookies and Bars; Pies
  Acorn Burritos, 64
  Flan de Calabaza, 185
  Mesquite Mousse, 81
  Pumpkin Cheesecake, 183
  Red Rice Pudding, 16
  Ruby Port Dessert, 11
Desserts, frozen
  Cactus Honey Sherbet, 12
  Harvest Ice Cream, 184
  Quick Saguaro Ice Cream, 31
  Saguaro Sherbet, 33
  Sunset Sherbet, 14
  Watercress Pineapple Snow, 120
Diet for a Small Planet (Lappé), 163
Distichlis palmeri, 214
Down Home Greens, 129
Dressed-Up Greens, 128
Dried Prickly Pears, 15
Dumplings
  Blue Corn, 166
  Trailside, 102
Dutch Oven Biscuits, 103

Egg Dishes
  Nopal Frittata, 19
  Tumbleweed Frittata, 124
  Wild Greens Soufflé, 132
  Winter Squash Soufflé, 178
Either Way Rosy Punch, 13
Elias-Cesnick, Anna, 211
Enchiladas
  Chile Cheese, 155
  Layered Tepary, 146
Energy Master Mix, 101
Energy Pancakes, 102

Environmental Research Laboratory,
  xv, 214
Epele, David, 6
Ewald, Ellen, 192

Felger, Richard S., xiv, 216
Felker, Pam, 75
Felker, Peter, 75
Fish and Seafood
  Callau, 91
  Salmon Nopalito Mousse, 21
  Sea of Cortez Gumbo, 22
Flan de Calabaza, 185
Fresh Corn Hominy, 168
Fresh Corn Pudding, 164
Fresh Mustard Salad, 115
Fritters, Squash Blossom, 175

Gazpacho Aspic, 18
Gelatin Dishes
  Gazpacho Aspic, 18
  Jellied Tumbleweed Salad, 123
  Mesquite Mousse, 81
  Ruby Port Dessert, 11
  Salmon Nopalito Mousse, 21
  Sweet and Sour Mold, 8
Gila Monster, 82
Global 2000 Report to the President,
  xiii
Golden Crepes, 206
Gourdola Bars, 199
Grandma's Honey Cookies, 100
Granola Brownies, 76
Green Beans, Sunny, 191
Green Chile Salsa, 154
Green Mayonnaise, 114
Greens and Yogurt Salad, 130
Greens in Artichoke Bottoms, 131
Greens Soufflé, Wild, 132
Greens Soup, Wild, 113
Gumbo, Sea of Cortez, 22
Guzman, Rafael, 161
Gyratory crusher, 70

Ham, in Callau, 91
Harvest Ice Cream, 184
Havasupai Indians, 116
Hayden, Julian, 70
Heiser, Charles, 187
Hi-Pro Breakfast Bars, 97